TRUTH LESSONS

Level One
Volume 4

Witness Lee

Living Stream Ministry
Anaheim, California

© 1987 Witness Lee

First Edition, 20,000 copies, May 1987.

Library of Congress Catalog
Card Number: 85-82564

ISBN 0-87083-282-4 (hardcover)
ISBN 0-87083-283-2 (softcover)
ISBN 0-87083-214-X (hardcover, four volume set)
ISBN 0-87083-213-1 (softcover, four volume set)

Published by

Living Stream Ministry
1853 W. Ball Road, P. O. Box 2121
Anaheim, CA 92804 U. S.A.

Printed in the United States of America

CONTENTS

TRUTH LESSONS—LEVEL ONE

REDEMPTION

(2)

WASHING

OUTLINE

I. The need for washing.

II. Positional washing:
   A. By the blood.
   B. Before God.
   C. In the believers' conscience.
   D. The washing of baptism.

III. Dispositional washing:
   A. In the name of the Lord Jesus Christ.
   B. In the Spirit.
   C. By faith.

IV. The result of being washed.

TEXT

This volume of *Truth Lessons* is a continuation of the preceding volume on the initial stage of God's full salvation. First, we will continue to see the different aspects of redemption. Immediately after we are forgiven of our sins and are freed, we are washed. God not only forgives us but also washes us. Forgiveness cancels the penalty for sins; washing removes all traces of sins. When God forgives us, He releases us from all responsibility for sin. When God washes us, He causes us to look as if we had never sinned.

I. THE NEED FOR WASHING

Man's sins not only make man a sinner with a charge against him before God, but they also cause him to become stained and defiled in himself. Therefore, man needs not only forgiveness but also washing.

Man is born of lust (Job 25:4-6), and his heart is defiled and filled with sins (Matt. 15:19-20). Hence, man is abominable and filthy. He delights in sinning and drinks iniquity like water (Job 15:14-16). Like a worm, he lives in uncleanness. There is none whose heart is clean and sinless, nor is there anyone who can make his heart clean and purify himself from sin (Prov. 20:9; 30:12). Furthermore, man has presented the members of his body as slaves to uncleanness (Rom. 6:19), causing them to become defiled. Man's mouth is full of cursing, blaspheming, judging, lying, obscenity, and foolish talking. Hence, man is of unclean lips and dwells in the midst of a people of unclean lips (Isa. 6:5).

Man's heart is filled with uncleanness and his mouth issues forth uncleanness; furthermore, man practices uncleanness, indulging in the lusts of his heart (Rom. 1:24). Men have all gone aside; together they are become filthy (Psa. 14:3). Hence, all men are unclean before God (Isa. 64:6). Like lepers, they are altogether unclean (Lev. 13:45) and truly need to be cleansed.

II. POSITIONAL WASHING

At the time we are saved, God applies to us the washing which the Lord Jesus accomplished. The washing which the Lord accomplished on the cross is an objective fact before God, and it is only carried out in us when we receive salvation.

The washing which we receive at the time we are saved is of two aspects. One aspect is the positional washing by the blood, and the other aspect is the dispositional washing by life. We receive both aspects of washing when we are saved through faith and baptism. Let us first look at the positional washing.

A. By the Blood

The uncleanness of the universe and of the human race comes from sin; hence, the redeeming blood is required for purification (Heb. 9:22). There first must be the shedding of blood for redemption from sins and then the blood can be used to wash the uncleanness of sin. The Lord Jesus shed His blood on the cross to accomplish redemption for our sins (1 Pet. 2:24) that His blood might purify us from the uncleanness of sin. Hence, the blood of Christ as a fountain for the washing of sins (Zech. 13:1) cleanses us at the time we believe into the Lord. This washing by the blood, which is outward and objective, is mainly before God for the washing of the uncleanness in our behavior. Although the Lord's blood also purifies our conscience within, this purification is for us to come forward to God with boldness (Heb. 10:19, 22).

B. Before God

Having shed His blood on the cross and having made purification of our sins once for all before God, the Lord Jesus sat down on the right hand of the Majesty on high (Heb. 1:3). He was not like the atoning priests in the old covenant, who could never sit down but needed to stand daily and offer often the same sacrifices (Heb. 10:11), because it was impossible for the blood of bulls and goats to take away sins (Heb. 10:4). But having offered one sacrifice for sins to take away our sin (John 1:29) and make purification of our sins forever, He sat down on the right hand of God (Heb. 10:10, 12). According to the type in Leviticus 16, He brought His blood into the Holy of Holies in the heavens and sprinkled it before God (Heb. 12:22, 24) to redeem us from sins, cleansing us of all sins before God. Once we believe that the Lord Jesus' death by the shedding of blood on the cross was for redeeming us from sins, His blood makes it possible for God to forgive us of our sins and to pardon us from the penalty of sin. At the same time, His blood also washes us from our sins before God, removing the stain of our sins (Rev. 1:5) and erasing all traces of our sins, so that we appear before God as if we had never sinned.

C. In the Believers' Conscience

When we believe and receive Christ, His blood also purifies our conscience (Heb. 9:14). According to the revelation of the Bible, the blood of Christ does not cleanse our heart; rather, it purifies our conscience. Our conscience is the most important part of our spirit, and our spirit is the organ by which we contact God. The conscience in our spirit enables us to hear God's voice and to know God's will. However, because we sinned, our conscience has been defiled and has lost its function. At the time we believe, God washes our sin-contaminated conscience with the Lord's redeeming blood, not only making it clean and transparent but also restoring its original function that through it we may serve God.

On the other hand, our conscience represents God and, in particular, God's law; that is, it reflects God and God's law. Whatever God condemns according to His law, our conscience also condemns and reflects (Rom. 2:14-15). Since the Lord's blood has satisfied God and the requirement of His law, it washes us from our sins, so that neither

God nor His law can condemn us any longer. Hence, our conscience, which represents both God and His law, also condemns us no longer because of the Lord's blood. Because the Lord's blood has washed away our sins before God and before His law, it also washes away our sins before our conscience. Such a conscience thus enables us to serve God with boldness.

D. The Washing of Baptism

The stain of our sins appears not only before God and in us, but also before men. Many of the ungodly and unrighteous things that we did in opposing God were done before men. Many sins that we committed and many evil, lustful, and filthy things that we did are known by the people around us. Therefore, at the time we believe and are saved, God uses another means to wash away the stain of sins which we have before men (Acts 22:16). This is the washing of baptism. Baptism is a silent declaration of our repentance unto God. Through baptism we declare to those around us the fact that we have repented and have believed and have been cleansed of the stain of our sins. Thus, we are loosed from the stain of sins which we have before men and become the repentant and washed ones in their eyes.

This is clearly illustrated in the Lord's sending of Ananias to find Saul and to baptize him (Acts 22:12-16). Formerly, Saul was one who opposed the Lord, persecuted the church, and ravaged the Christians. This was a fact known to all, especially to the Christians. Now that he had been met by the Lord and had repented unto Him, he should be baptized that people might know that this one who had formerly opposed the Lord and had persecuted the church had now turned to the Lord and become a Christian, so that his sin of opposing God and of persecuting the church might be washed away before men.

III. DISPOSITIONAL WASHING

Not only are we defiled in our behavior before God, but

we are also unclean inwardly in our nature. Our outward behavior is defiled, and our inward nature is unclean. Therefore, the washing that God has prepared for us in His salvation consists not only of the positional aspect but also of the dispositional aspect. The positional aspect stresses the removing of the defilement in our behavior before God, before His law, and before our conscience. The dispositional aspect emphasizes the removing of the defilement inwardly in our nature. Hence, the dispositional washing is absolutely subjective; it is an inward washing.

A. In the Name of the Lord Jesus Christ

First, we are washed in life dispositionally in the name of the Lord Jesus Christ (1 Cor. 6:11). Being washed in the name of the Lord Jesus Christ denotes being washed in the person of the Lord, in the Lord Himself, that is, in the organic union with the Lord by faith. When we call on the Lord Jesus, we experience the living person of the Lord, we are in Him, and we have an organic union with Him, sharing His life and nature. His life and His nature cause us to be delivered from our unclean life and defiled nature, that is, from our dispositional defilement. Hence, we are washed dispositionally in the name of the Lord Jesus Christ, in the living person of the Lord.

B. In the Spirit

We are washed dispositionally not only in the name of the Lord Jesus but also in the Spirit (1 Cor. 6:11), that all defilement may be removed from our entire being and that we may be cleansed. The name of the Lord Jesus is His living person, and His person is the Spirit. When we call on the Lord Jesus, He comes to us as the Spirit. This Spirit is the Spirit of life (Rom. 8:2), in whom God transfuses His divine life to us. Through this life we are freed from our natural disposition and from the life that we had originally. Therefore, through this life we are also loosed from the defilement of our natural disposition and from the filthiness of our original life that we may be washed in life dispositionally.

C. By Faith

We are washed dispositionally by faith. In His saving way God does not cleanse our heart with the redeeming blood of Christ, but He does cleanse our heart with His Spirit of life through our union with the Lord by faith (Acts 15:9). This means that our old heart, which is desperately wicked and incurable (Jer. 17:9), filled with all kinds of defilement (Matt. 15:18-20), and hard as stone, is changed into a new heart (Ezek. 36:26), which is clean and pliable, that we may be purified in our heart. Hence, we are washed in life dispositionally by faith.

IV. THE RESULT OF BEING WASHED

The result of God's washing is that we become as white as snow and as wool before God (Isa. 1:18). Snow and wool are naturally white. Therefore, this tells us that as a result of God's washing we become not only white but naturally white, as if we had never been defiled. Furthermore, God's washing not only makes us as white as snow but even whiter than snow (Psa. 51:7). What a washing!

God's washing also results in our being made inwardly pure and without blemish both in life and in nature as He is.

SUMMARY

Man's sins not only make man a sinner with a charge against him before God, but they cause him to become stained and defiled in himself. Therefore, man needs not only forgiveness but also washing. The washing which we receive at the time we are saved is of two aspects: positional washing and dispositional washing. The positional washing by the blood is through the redeeming blood of Christ. This blood cleanses us at the time we believe into the Lord. This washing, which is outward and objective, is mainly before God for the washing of the uncleanness in our behavior. The blood also cleanses our conscience that we may come forward to God with boldness to serve Him with a pure conscience. Positional washing also includes the washing of baptism. Through baptism we declare to those around us the fact that we have repented and have believed and have been cleansed of the stain of our sins, so that we become the repentant and washed ones in their eyes. Dispositional washing emphasizes the removing of the defilement inwardly in our nature. We are washed in life dispositionally in the name of the Lord Jesus Christ and in the Spirit through faith, that we may be loosed from the defilement of our original life and nature and be washed in life dispositionally. The result of God's washing is that before God we become as white as snow, even whiter than snow, just as if we had never sinned. Furthermore, we are also made inwardly pure and without blemish both in life and in nature as He is.

QUESTIONS

1. Briefly explain the need for washing.
2. Briefly explain the positional washing by the blood.
3. Briefly explain the washing of baptism.
4. How do believers receive the dispositional washing of life?
5. What is the result of being washed?

REDEMPTION

(3)

SANCTIFICATION

OUTLINE

I. The meaning of sanctification.

II. The way to be sanctified:
   A. By faith in Christ.
   B. By being in Christ.

III. Positional sanctification:
   A. By Christ's offering one sacrifice.
   B. By the blood of Jesus.
   C. By being called.

IV. Dispositional sanctification:
   A. By Him who sanctifies.
   B. In the name of the Lord Jesus Christ.
   C. In the Spirit.

V. The means of sanctification:
   A. The life—Christ.
   B. The light—the Bible.
   C. The power—the Holy Spirit.

TEXT

In this lesson we will cover another aspect of redemption, that is, sanctification. In Lesson Twenty-nine we saw that the Spirit sanctifies us unto repentance. After we have been forgiven of our sins and washed, God continues to sanctify us. Sanctification, or being made holy, is an important part of God's salvation. Concerning the matter of sanctification, the Bible not only speaks a great deal, but it speaks with great clarity. In this lesson we will see what sanctification is according to the Scriptures.

I. THE MEANING OF SANCTIFICATION

Sanctification, whether in the Hebrew language of the Old Testament or in the Greek language of the New Testament, means primarily separation. Therefore, sanctification, or being made holy, in the Scriptures means separation from what is ordinary or common.

Holiness is the quality of God's nature. The quality of God's nature is not merely to be sinless, without any defilement, but it is even more to be different, distinct, from everything common. Therefore, the Bible speaks of God and the things pertaining or belonging to God as being holy. A certain thing is not holy until it is offered to God and belongs to God. Only then is it sanctified, separated. A bull or a goat, for example, is not intrinsically holy, but when it is placed on the altar, it is made holy (Matt. 23:19), because the altar separates it unto God. Gold is not holy in itself, but it is sanctified when it is placed in the temple (Matt. 23:17), because the temple separates it unto God. Food is not intrinsically holy, but it is sanctified through the saints' prayer, because the saints' prayer separates the food for the use of the saints of God (1 Tim. 4:4-5). Bulls, goats, gold, and food are in the world, of the world, and for the world. Hence, they are common, not holy. But the altar has separated some bulls or goats, the temple has separated some gold, and the saints' intercession has separated some food. When these things are separated, they are unto God, of God, and directly or indirectly for God. Hence, they are sanctified. To sanctify a certain thing is not to make it sinless but to separate it unto God. A bull, a goat, gold, and food do not have the problem of sin, but they do have the problem of the world. Although they are not evil, they are common. They belong to the world and they are for the people in the world; they are not to God or for God. Hence, they need to be sanctified, that is, to be separated unto God and to be for God. Not only do they need to be separated from sin, but even more they need to be separated from the world, from worldliness, and from everything that is not of God or for God, that they may be sanctified unto God and correspond to the quality of God's holy nature.

Leviticus 10:10 says, "... make a distinction between the holy and the common ..." (ASV). This indicates that the opposite of "holy" is not "sinful" but "common." To be holy is to be distinct from what is common. Something which is common or ordinary may not be faulty or sinful, but it is not holy because it is not separated. A person may behave so well that in man's eyes he is irreproachable and perfect, yet he is still common, not holy. Although he is well-behaved, he is common, ordinary, not separated from the common, the ordinary; he is, therefore, not sanctified unto God. Although he does not do evil as others do, he follows the tide of the world and walks according to the world. Hence, although he is well-behaved, he still needs to be sanctified. This is because sanctification not only separates us from wickedness and defilement but also makes us distinct from that which is common.

To be sanctified, on the negative side, is to be separated from all things other than God; on the positive side, it is to be separated unto God. Everything outside of God is common; only God and everything belonging to God are holy. All persons, matters, and things are outside of God and are worldly; hence, they are common. Sanctification is

to separate these common persons, matters, and things
from everything outside of God that they may be unto God
and of God. Since God alone is holy, only that which is
unto God and of God is holy.

II. THE WAY TO BE SANCTIFIED

A. By Faith in Christ

To be holy, to be separated unto God, we must
first believe into Christ (Acts 26:18). Christ offered Himself
as the sacrifice to redeem us from our sins, shedding His blood to repurchase us (1 Cor. 6:20; Acts 20:28),
that we may be sanctified (Heb. 13:12). If we desire to
participate in this fact, we must believe into Him (Acts
26:18), that is, we must be joined to Him by faith. When we
believe into Him, when we are joined to Him by faith,
we are sanctified through His redemption. We have
sanctification in fact, sanctification in position. Hence,
the way for us to be sanctified is by believing into
Christ.

B. By Being in Christ

When we believe into Christ, we enter into Him and are
joined to Him. Because He is holy (Luke 1:35; Acts 2:27;
1 John 2:20), when we are in Him and are joined to Him, we
are separated, sanctified (1 Cor. 1:2). Christ is the element
and sphere that separates us, makes us holy, unto God.
Therefore, the way for us to be sanctified is also by being
in Christ.

III. POSITIONAL SANCTIFICATION

The sanctification we receive in God's salvation is of
two aspects, positional sanctification and dispositional
sanctification. Positional sanctification is a fact which we
receive in Christ when we believe. When we believe, we
may not immediately have the experience of subjective
sanctification, but we do receive the fact of sanctification,
that is, we are sanctified positionally.

A. By Christ's Offering One Sacrifice

We were forever sanctified at the time we were redeemed through Christ's offering of His body on the cross as the one sacrifice for sins (Heb. 10:10). When Christ offered Himself to God, He took away our sin (John 1:29) and accomplished the purification of sins once for all (Heb. 1:3; 7:27; 9:26). Once we were far off from God because of sin, but through His redemption Christ has delivered us from sin and has brought us back to God to be separated unto Him forever. This is the positional sanctification which we have received in God's salvation.

B. By the Blood of Jesus

We are sanctified positionally because of the blood of Jesus. By His own blood the Lord Jesus has found an eternal redemption for us (Heb. 9:12) and has purchased us back to God (1 Cor. 6:20; Acts 20:28; 1 Pet. 1:18-19; Rev. 5:9). Thus, He has sanctified us (Heb. 13:12), making us distinct from the worldly people. Therefore, when we were purchased back by the Lord with His blood, we were sanctified in fact, in position; that is, in God's eyes we were separated, sanctified, unto Him.

C. By Being Called

We are sanctified positionally by being called. God's calling is to call us out from among the worldly people unto God Himself. Therefore, when we were called, we were separated, sanctified, and we became the called saints (1 Cor. 1:2; Rom. 1:7). Not only Paul and Peter were saints, but we, the saved ones, also are saints. We are those who are sanctified unto God.

IV. DISPOSITIONAL SANCTIFICATION

Sanctification is not only a matter of position, but it is also a matter of disposition in that God imparts His nature into us that we may partake of His divine nature (2 Pet. 1:4).

A. By Him Who Sanctifies

We are sanctified dispositionally by Him who sanctifies. Hebrews 2:11 says, "For both He who sanctifies and those who are being sanctified are all of one." This indicates that Christ as the Sanctifier and we as the sanctified are all out of one source, one Father. God the Father is not only the source of the Sanctifier, but He is also the source of all who are being sanctified by Christ. Christ and we are all out of one Father, one source. He and we have the same life (Col. 3:4) and nature. This clearly reveals that sanctification in this sense does not concern position but disposition.

In order to be the One who sanctifies us positionally, Christ needed to pass through the process of incarnation, crucifixion, resurrection, glorification, and exaltation. Before His incarnation, Christ was the only begotten Son of God, having only the divine nature but not the human nature. Hence, He could not be the Sanctifier to sanctify us dispositionally. When He was incarnated, on the one hand, He was still the only begotten Son of God; on the other hand, He put on human nature. Although the divine nature within Him was the Son of God, His human nature was not, because His human part was not yet born of God. Hence, He could not be the Sanctifier to sanctify us dispositionally. He needed to pass through death and resurrection in order for His human part to be born of God and for Him to become the firstborn Son of God (Acts 13:33), having both the divine nature and the human nature. Furthermore, through His joining Himself to us, we have been regenerated of God to become the many sons of God, having both the divine nature and the human nature as He does. Therefore, He can be our Sanctifier to make us as holy dispositionally as He is.

B. In the Name of the Lord Jesus Christ

We are sanctified dispositionally by being in the name of the Lord Jesus Christ. First Corinthians 6:11 says, "But you were sanctified...in the name of the Lord Jesus Christ." Sanctification here is not the objective aspect which we receive positionally through the blood; it is the subjective aspect which we experience dispositionally in the name of the Lord. In the New Testament, to be in the name of the Lord Jesus Christ is to be in His person, in an organic union with Him through faith; in reality, it is to be in Christ Himself. When we call on the Lord Jesus, we are in His name, in the living person of Christ. We have an organic union with Him, participating in His divine life and nature. Thus, we are sanctified dispositionally.

C. In the Spirit

We are sanctified dispositionally also by being in the Spirit. According to 1 Corinthians 6:11, we have been sanctified not only in the name of the Lord Jesus Christ but also in the Spirit of God. The name of the Lord Jesus Christ is His person, and His person is the Spirit. Hence, the Lord's name and His Spirit are inseparable. When we call on the name of the Lord, the Lord reaches us as the Spirit. This Spirit is the Spirit of holiness (Rom. 1:4). Therefore, when we are joined to the Lord, we experience the sanctifying work of the Spirit and receive the subjective sanctification in our disposition.

V. THE MEANS OF SANCTIFICATION

A. The Life—Christ

First Corinthians 1:30 says, "...Christ Jesus, who became wisdom to us from God:...sanctification...." This indicates that sanctification is Christ. At the time of our believing, Christ enters into us to be our life. This life is holy, and it imparts His holy nature into us. Thus, we are sanctified and are able to live out a sanctified life.

B. The Light—the Bible

In order to sanctify us, God has given us not only His

life within but also the Bible without. The Bible is the Word of God, and the Word of God is the truth, which can sanctify us (John 17:17). Inwardly, the life of Christ imparts to us the holy nature and taste. Outwardly, the truth of the Bible becomes our sanctifying light and guidance. The inward life demands that we be holy; the outward truth teaches us to be sanctified. The holy nature within responds to the sanctifying light without, and the sanctifying guidance without stimulates the holy taste within. These two, one within and the other without, echo, cooperate with, and complement one another.

C. The Power—the Holy Spirit

In order to make us holy, not only has God given us Christ to be the sanctifying life within and the Bible to be the sanctifying light without, but He has also given us the Holy Spirit to be the sanctifying power, so that by Him we may be sanctified (Rom. 15:16; 1 Cor. 6:11; 2 Thes. 2:13). The Holy Spirit not only increases the demands of the holy life within and intensifies the shining of the holy truth without, but He also becomes our power enabling us to answer the inward demands of the holy life and to obey the outward enlightening of the holy truth. Combined together like three strands of a string, these three—the life of Christ, the light of the Bible, and the power of the Holy Spirit—make it possible for us to live according to the divine nature, that is, in the divine nature, and thus become those who are sanctified.

SUMMARY

Sanctification, or being made holy, means separation from what is ordinary or common. Holiness is the quality of God's nature. The quality of God's nature is not merely to be sinless, without any defilement, but it is even more to be different, distinct, from everything common. When God sanctifies us, He separates us not only from sin, but even more from the world, from worldliness, and from everything that is not of God or for God, that we may be separated unto God and correspond to the quality of God's holy nature. To be holy, we must believe into Christ to participate in the fact that He has shed His blood to repurchase us that we may be sanctified. Furthermore, we must enter into Him and be joined to Him. Only then can we be holy as He is. Such sanctification is of two aspects, the positional aspect and the dispositional aspect. Positional sanctification is accomplished by Christ's offering Himself as the one sacrifice and redeeming us by His own blood, thus forever sanctifying us unto God. It is also accomplished by God's calling, which calls us out from among the worldly people, thus sanctifying us unto God Himself. Dispositional sanctification is through the Sanctifier, Christ. Through Him we who have been regenerated of God to become the many sons of God, having both the divine nature and the human nature as He does, receive the subjective, dispositional sanctification. By Christ as the sanctifying life, the Bible as the sanctifying light, and the Holy Spirit as the sanctifying power, we can live according to the divine nature, that is, in the divine nature, and thus become those who are sanctified.

QUESTIONS

1. Briefly explain the meaning of sanctification.
2. Briefly discuss the way to be sanctified.
3. Briefly explain how man can be sanctified positionally.
4. Briefly explain how man can be sanctified dispositionally.
5. Briefly discuss the three means by which the believers may live out a sanctified life.

LESSON THIRTY-NINE

REDEMPTION

(4)

JUSTIFICATION

OUTLINE

I. Man not justified by works.

II. Objective justification:
   A. By God's grace.
   B. Through the redemption in Christ Jesus.
   C. By faith in Christ:
      1. Faith being the way to be justified.
      2. Faith being Christ Himself.
   D. To receive the righteousness of God.
   E. Evidenced:
      1. By the resurrection of Christ.
      2. By the ascension of Christ.

III. Subjective justification:
   A. By the divine life.
   B. By Christ in His resurrection.
   C. In the name of the Lord Jesus Christ.
   D. In the Spirit.

TEXT

In this lesson we shall cover another aspect of redemption, that is, justification. After the believers are forgiven, freed, washed, and sanctified, they have no more problems before God. Hence, God has the position, the ground, to justify them. In the Bible, justification means that God, according to His righteousness, declares that man is righteous. Therefore, when God justifies man, He justifies man according to His standard of righteousness.

I. MAN NOT JUSTIFIED BY WORKS

Since justification means that God, according to His righteousness, declares that man is righteous, how can man be justified by God through his own works? God's righteousness is perfect and supreme. But no one is perfect in works before the law of God. The Bible, therefore, definitely tells us that by the works of law no flesh shall be justified before God (Rom. 3:20; Gal. 2:16). Man's righteousnesses simply cannot stand before the righteousness of God; they are even like a filthy garment (Isa. 64:6), being unable either to match the requirement of God's righteousness or be justified before God. Therefore, man can never be justified by works before God.

II. OBJECTIVE JUSTIFICATION

A. By God's Grace

Man is justified first by God's grace. Because of man's own weakness, no one can be justified before God by works of law. Everyone, however, can be justified by the grace of God (Rom. 3:24; Titus 3:7). Justification by law requires man to be perfect. This is a requirement which no one can meet. Justification by grace is God's approving man by fulfilling for man freely all the requirements of His righteousness. This is a gift we all can receive and obtain. Because God has done everything that we may be justified freely, there is no need for us to do anything, neither to use any effort nor pay any price. God has done it all for us. Hence, this is grace. What we cannot obtain by law we can receive by grace.

B. Through the Redemption in Christ Jesus

We are justified by God's grace through the redemption in Christ Jesus (Rom. 3:24). If the Lord Jesus had not shed His blood on the cross and accomplished redemption to satisfy all the requirements of God's righteousness for us, God would have no ground and no way to justify us by His grace even if He desired to do so. Hence, without the redemption in the Lord Jesus, the grace by which God justifies us cannot reach us. The Lord Jesus, however, has shed His precious blood and paid the price on the cross, thus satisfying all the requirements of God's righteousness (Rom. 5:9). Therefore, God can justify us by His grace according to His righteousness that we may be justified according to His standard of righteousness.

C. By Faith in Christ

Man is justified by God's grace through the redemption in Christ Jesus and also by believing into Christ.

1. Faith Being the Way to Be Justified

The Bible clearly and definitely indicates that a man is not and cannot be justified before God by works; he is and can only be justified by faith (Gal. 3:8; 2:16; Rom. 3:22, 28; Acts 13:39). "By works" is to rely on our own doing, whereas "by faith" is to trust in what Christ has done for us. "Works" require our effort to do, to perform; "faith" is our receiving, obtaining, without effort. No one has the strength to do, but everyone can believe.

Acts 13:39 says, "And from all things from which you could not be justified by the law of Moses, in this One [Christ] everyone who believes is justified." Christ has died for us and shed His blood to accomplish redemption, satisfying God's righteous demand, so that God can justify us according to His righteousness. But if we do not believe, Christ and what He has done have nothing to do with us, and we still cannot be justified by God. Therefore, we must be joined to Christ through faith; we must believe into Him and by faith receive Him and what He has done for us. Only then can we participate in Him and in His redemption, and only then can we be in Him and be justified through His redemption.

2. Faith Being Christ Himself

Galatians 2:16b says, "We also have believed in Christ Jesus that we might be justified by the faith of Christ." The expression "the faith of Christ" shows that our faith comes from Christ. We are justified by the faith of Christ. The faith of Christ is actually Christ Himself, who has entered into us as our believing element and ability. Such faith is reckoned to us as righteousness by God (Rom. 4:22-24). Therefore, genuine believing is to believe into Christ by His faith. He is the source, the cause, of our faith (Heb. 12:2).

According to our natural man, we do not have any believing ability. We do not have faith by ourselves. It is when we read the Bible or hear a gospel preacher preaching this all-inclusive Christ according to the Bible, that the Holy Spirit causes us to see the revelation of the all-inclusive person and work of Christ through the word of the Bible. That is, by showing us the divine scenery, the Holy Spirit causes the knowledge and appreciation of Christ to be generated in us, thus producing in us the trust in Christ. This is Christ's infusing Himself into us to be the faith in us. This faith is reckoned by God as the believers' righteousness. God reckons this kind of faith as a righteous deed. In ourselves we do not have any righteousness, and before God we do not have any righteous deed. But if we take God's word, stand on it, and obey it, and if we believe into His Son Jesus Christ, God will count this kind of faith as our righteousness. Therefore, we simply need to repent and call on the Lord, saying, "O Lord Jesus, I believe in You." God will regard this as the highest righteousness, and we shall be justified by God. This is a matter of our being justified objectively by faith.

D. To Receive the Righteousness of God

When we are justified by God's grace, through the redemption in Christ Jesus, and by believing into Christ, we receive the righteousness of God (Rom. 3:22; 1:17; Phil. 3:9). Romans 3:22 says, "Even the righteousness of God through faith of Jesus Christ to all those who believe." Hence, when we believe by the faith of Jesus Christ, we not only are justified by God, but we also receive the righteousness of God. The righteousness of God is what God is, God's attribute, with respect to justice and uprightness. God is just and upright. Whatever God is in His justice and uprightness constitutes His righteousness. Furthermore, all that God is in His justice and uprightness is actually Himself in His acts and actions. Since God is also embodied in Christ (Col. 2:9), the righteousness of God is simply Christ. Therefore, when we receive the righteousness of God, we receive Christ Himself as our righteousness (1 Cor. 1:30). Just as He is righteous before God and justified by God, so we are also righteous before God and justified by God in Him.

E. Evidenced

1. By the Resurrection of Christ

Romans 4:25 says, "Who [Jesus]...was raised because of our justification." This shows that the resurrection of Christ proves that we are justified; it is an evidence of our justification. The death of Christ fully fulfilled and satisfied God's righteous requirements so that we may be fully justified by God through Christ's death. Christ's resurrection was God's vindication and approval of His work, and it was also a sign of His universal success. His rising up from among the dead was a sign indicating that what He had done prior to His death was successful and that it has an eternal efficacy in His resurrection. Therefore, His resurrection proves that His death has satisfied God forever, and that through His death God can fully justify us. Hence, Christ's resurrection is an evidence that we have been justified by God.

2. By the Ascension of Christ

John 16:10 says, "And concerning righteousness, because I [Christ] go to the Father." Therefore, Christ's ascending to the Father after His death and resurrection is also a proof of the believers' justification. Stanza three of *Hymns*, #20 says,

> Father God, Thou hast accepted
> Jesus as our Substitute;
> Judged the Just One for the unjust,
> Couldst Thou change Thy attitude?
> As a proof of perfect justice,
> At Thine own right hand He sits;
> He, as Thy full satisfaction,
> Righteously Thy need befits.

Thus, the resurrected Christ who sits at the right hand of God is also an evidence that we have been justified. The redeeming death of Christ as the ground for God to justify us has been fully accepted by God and has fully satisfied God. And, as a proof of this, Christ has been resurrected from the dead and has ascended to the right hand of God, thus demonstrating the fact that God has justified us through His death.

III. SUBJECTIVE JUSTIFICATION

A. By the Divine Life

We have been justified objectively, positionally, by God's grace, through the redemption of Christ Jesus, and by our faith. Hence, we can be justified unto life (Rom.

5:18) subjectively by the divine life. The result of positional justification is that we have the position to receive the divine life. This life is working in us to make us righteous in every matter. Objective justification alters our outward position so that we may be justified by God and be reconciled to Him; subjective justification changes our inward nature so that our living may be justified by God.

B. By Christ in His Resurrection

Furthermore, we are justified subjectively by Christ in His resurrection. Romans 4:25 says, "Who [Jesus]...was raised because of our justification." This indicates that, on the one hand, Christ's resurrection is the proof of our outward, objective justification; on the other hand, the resurrected Christ enters into us that we may have the subjective justification. This resurrected Christ is living in us now to be our life (Col. 1:27b; 3:4a) that we may live out a life of righteousness. This is not the objective, positional justification which we have received through Christ's redemption; rather, this is the subjective, dispositional justification which we obtain through Christ's life. Outwardly, His blood brings us the objective justification; inwardly, His resurrection life brings us the subjective justification. Objective justification is by our believing into Him; subjective justification is by our living by Him. Therefore, God not only has the position outwardly to justify us, but He also can make us righteous by the resurrection life of Christ in us.

C. In the Name of the Lord Jesus Christ

We are justified subjectively in the name of the Lord Jesus Christ. First Corinthians 6:11 says, "But you were justified in the name of the Lord Jesus Christ." To be in the name of the Lord Jesus Christ is to be in the person of Jesus Christ, that is, in Jesus Christ Himself. This tells us of the believers' organic union with the Lord. When we call on the Lord Jesus, we have an organic union with Him in

His name, in His living person, and we also participate in His divine life and nature. Thus, we are justified subjectively.

D. In the Spirit

Moreover, we are justified subjectively in the Spirit. First Corinthians 6:11 continues, "You were justified in the name of the Lord Jesus Christ and in the Spirit of our God." Therefore, we experience the subjective justification in the name of the Lord and in the Spirit of God. The Lord's name denotes the Lord's person. The Lord in resurrection now is the Spirit (2 Cor. 3:17). Therefore, we cannot separate the Lord's name from His Spirit. When we have an organic union with Him in His name, we participate in and enjoy the resurrected Christ as life in the Spirit. Thus, we are justified subjectively.

SUMMARY

God's justification is God's declaring that man is righteous according to His righteousness. Hence, no one can be justified by his own works. The believers' justification consists of the objective aspect and the subjective aspect. We receive the objective justification freely by God's grace, through the redemption in Christ Jesus, and by our faith. Faith is the way for us to be justified, and our faith comes from Christ, who is the source, the cause, of our faith. When He enters into us to be our believing element and ability, this faith is reckoned to us as righteousness by God. When we are justified by God, we receive God's righteousness; that is, we receive Christ Himself as our righteousness so that we are righteous before God and are justified by God just as Christ is. The evidences of our justification are the resurrection and ascension of Christ. He has risen from among the dead and has ascended to the right hand of God. This proves that His redeeming death has been fully accepted by God and has completely satisfied God; God can fully justify us through His death. We are justified subjectively by the divine life, by Christ in resurrection, in the name of the Lord Jesus Christ, and in the Spirit. Because the resurrected Christ is the Spirit, when we call on Him, we have an organic union with Him. Thus, we are able to participate in and enjoy Him as our life that we may live out righteousness by Him and thereby be justified subjectively.

QUESTIONS

1. Why is man not justified by works?

2. How do the believers receive objective justification?

3. Quote the Scriptures to prove that faith is Christ Himself and explain briefly what this means.

4. What are the evidences of the believers' justification?

5. How do the believers receive subjective justification?

REDEMPTION

(5)

RECONCILIATION

OUTLINE

I. The need for reconciliation:
   A. Man being an enemy of God.
   B. Man being at enmity with God in his mind.
   C. Man disapproving of holding God in his knowledge.
   D. Man hating and blaspheming God.
   E. Man being a son of disobedience and a child of wrath.

II. The accomplishment of reconciliation:
   A. Through Christ.
   B. Through the death of Christ with the shedding of His blood.

III. The ministry of reconciliation.

IV. The results of reconciliation:
   A. Having peace toward God.
   B. Boasting in God.
   C. Being saved in life.

V. The relationship between reconciliation and propitiation:
   A. The meaning of propitiation.
   B. Reconciliation including propitiation.

TEXT

In this lesson we shall cover the last aspect of redemption, that is, reconciliation to God. Through Christ's redemption, we not only have been forgiven, freed, washed, sanctified, and justified, but we also have been reconciled to God. The phrase "reconciliation to God" in Greek means to have a thorough change toward God. Because of the fall, man disobeyed God, offended God, and became an enemy of God. Therefore, man needs to have a thorough change toward God through Christ's redemption. Our having a thorough change toward God is our being reconciled to God. The Bible does not say that God is reconciled to us; it only says that we are reconciled to God. Because He never offended us, God does not need to be reconciled to us. It is we who offended Him; hence, we need to be reconciled to Him.

I. THE NEED FOR RECONCILIATION

A. Man Being an Enemy of God

Man needs to be reconciled to God because man is an enemy of God. Romans 5:10a says, "For if, while we were enemies, we were reconciled to God through the death of His Son." This indicates that before man receives God's salvation, in God's eyes he is not only a sinner but also an enemy of God. Through the fall, man not only has fallen into sin, but he also has fallen under the authority of Satan (1 John 5:19). Hence, he has become a child of the Devil (1 John 3:8a, 10), obeying the ruler of the authority of the air (Eph. 2:2). Being hostile to God, he has also become an enemy of God. Therefore, man needs not only to be forgiven by God but also to be reconciled to God.

B. Man Being at Enmity with God in His Mind

Man needs to be reconciled to God also because he is at enmity with God in his mind. Colossians 1:21 says, "And you, who once were alienated and enemies in your mind by evil works." Because of the fall, man not only is far off and alienated from God, but he also is at enmity with God in his mind by evil works. Furthermore, the mind of fallen man is set on the evil flesh. Such a mind is hated by God and it is enmity against God (Rom. 8:5, 7). Hence, man needs not only to repent unto God and be forgiven, but also to be reconciled to God.

C. Man Disapproving of Holding God in His Knowledge

Man needs to be reconciled to God because he disapproves of holding God in his knowledge. Romans 1:28a says, "And as they...did not approve of holding God in their full knowledge." Man is alienated from God to the extent that he disapproves of holding God in his knowledge. In Greek, this means that man does not think it good to have God in his knowledge. Therefore, it is not that man cannot know God; rather, it is that man disapproves of holding God in his knowledge—he does not think it good to have God in his knowledge. Man intentionally refuses to know God, purposely puts God aside, and deliberately rejects God. Therefore, man needs to be reconciled to God.

D. Man Hating and Blaspheming God

Man needs to be reconciled to God because he hates God and blasphemes God. Romans 1:30 shows us that fallen man hates God. In 1 Timothy 1:13 Paul tells us that before he believed in the Lord he was one who blasphemed God. Hatred is the inward intention; blasphemy is the outward word and conduct. Man hates God in his inward mind and intent, and he blasphemes God in his outward words and behavior. First, man is at enmity with God in his heart, and, disapproving of God, he does not think it good to have God in his knowledge. Then he hates God in his heart and thus blasphemes God outwardly. Man therefore truly needs to be reconciled to God.

E. Man Being a Son of Disobedience and a Child of Wrath

Man needs to be reconciled to God because he is a son of disobedience and a child of wrath. Ephesians 2:2-3 shows us that before God fallen men are sons of disobedience and children of wrath. Because of their rebellion against God and their resistance to God, fallen men are sons of disobedience. Hence, they have incurred God's righteous anger and are children of wrath who are under God's wrath. Since man's relationship with God has fallen to such a state, he truly needs to be redeemed and reconciled to God that he may have a thorough change toward God.

II. THE ACCOMPLISHMENT OF RECONCILIATION

Although man rejects God, hates God, and is at enmity with God, God loves man and delights in man. Man does not want God, yet God wants man. Man has offended God and needs to be reconciled to God, yet man does not have the thought of being reconciled to God, much less has he found a way to be reconciled to God. Although God has never offended man and does not need to be reconciled to man, He desires that man would be reconciled to Him, and He even accomplished a way of propitiation that man may be reconciled to Himself. This is because He loves man and delights in man.

A. Through Christ

God has reconciled us to Himself in Christ, that is, through Christ. Second Corinthians 5:18-19 says, "God, who has reconciled us to Himself through Christ...; how that God was in Christ reconciling the world to Himself." This clearly indicates that God accomplished reconciliation in Christ, that is, through Christ. "In Christ" indicates that Christ is the instrument and the sphere in which God has reconciled us. Although God loves us and desires that we would be reconciled to Him, it is only in the sphere of Christ and through Christ that we can be reconciled to God. Therefore, it is in Christ, that is, through Christ, that God has reconciled us to Himself.

B. Through the Death of Christ with the Shedding of His Blood

Moreover, God has reconciled us to Himself through the death of Christ with the shedding of His blood. Colossians 1:20 and 22 say, "And through Him to reconcile all things to Him, having made peace through the blood of His cross...yet now has He reconciled in the body of His flesh through death." In order that we might be reconciled to Him, God accomplished a propitiatory way for us, which is the redemption of Christ. Christ died for our sins and shed His blood on the cross to accomplish redemption that we might be reconciled to God. Because the redemption of Christ has solved all the problems and removed all the barriers between us and God, and because it has satisfied the demand of God's righteousness, holiness, and glory, we can turn back to God and be reconciled to Him, and God can also receive us and be pleased with us.

III. THE MINISTRY OF RECONCILIATION

Second Corinthians 5:18 says, "...and has given to us the ministry of reconciliation." In order that the world might be reconciled to Himself, God accomplished all the necessary steps of reconciliation through Christ. Not only so, He also has given to men the ministry of reconciliation, so that they may become ambassadors of Christ, commissioned to represent Him for reconciling people to God. God is anxiously hoping that we may be reconciled to Him. So urgent is this matter to Him that He sends men to us, entreating and beseeching us to be reconciled to Him. Hence, if we still are not reconciled to God, the problem is not with Him but with us. The problem is that we would not accept God's love or listen to His

entreating, nor would we respond to His beseeching and be
reconciled to Him.

IV. THE RESULTS OF RECONCILIATION

A. Having Peace toward God

The first result of our reconciliation to God is that we
have peace toward God (Rom. 5:1); that is, we are walking
toward God on the way of peace. Formerly, as sinners we
had no peace; neither did we know the way of peace (Rom.
3:17). Since we have been reconciled to God and have peace
toward God, we are walking on the way of peace. This is
an issue of our reconciliation to God.

B. Boasting in God

As a result of our reconciliation to God, we can boast in
God. Romans 5:11 says, "We also are boasting in God
through our Lord Jesus Christ, through whom we have
now received the reconciliation." The word boast in Greek
also means exult and glory. Since we have been reconciled
to God through the Lord Jesus Christ, we boast, exult, and
glory in God. Because we have been reconciled to God and
have received God, God Himself has become our eternal
portion. We enjoy Him, and we boast, exult, and glory in
Him, even in tribulations (Rom. 5:3). We also boast in hope
of the glory of God (Rom. 5:2). This also is an issue of our
reconciliation to God.

C. Being Saved in Life

As a result of our reconciliation to God, we are being
saved in life (Rom. 5:10). When we are reconciled to God,
have peace toward Him, enjoy Him, and boast in Him, we
are being saved in His life. We are being saved from so
many negative things and freed from besetting sins, from
the world and its usurpation, from our temper, disposition,
self, and natural being, and from being individualistic.
This salvation in life also is an issue of our reconciliation
to God.

V. THE RELATIONSHIP BETWEEN
RECONCILIATION AND PROPITIATION

A. The Meaning of Propitiation

The Greek word for propitiation means to conciliate two parties and make them one. Suppose you have a problem with another person. You have either offended him or else you owe him something. Because of this problem or debt, he has a demand upon you, and unless his demand is satisfied, the problem between you and him cannot be resolved, nor can reconciliation be achieved. Thus, there is the need for propitiation. The problem that kept us from God, that made it impossible for us to fellowship with Him, was our sins. Our sins kept us away from God's presence and hindered God from coming to us. Therefore, we needed propitiation to appease God's demands.

In 1 John 2:2 and 4:10 we are told that Christ, the Son of God, is Himself the propitiation concerning our sins. In both places the word propitiation in Greek is *hilasmos*, which means "that which propitiates," that is, a propitiatory sacrifice. Romans 3:25 says that God set forth Christ Jesus as a propitiation-cover. The word translated "propitiation-cover" is another Greek word regarding propitiation, *hilasterion*, which means the place where propitiation was made. In the Septuagint, *hilasterion* is used in Exodus 25 and Leviticus 16 for the cover of the ark, the place where God granted mercy to man; hence, it is called the mercy seat (Exo. 25:17; Lev. 16:2). Furthermore, Hebrews 2:17 says that the Lord Jesus became the High Priest to make propitiation for the sins of the people. Here, "make propitiation for" in Greek is *hilaskomai*, the verbal form of the noun *hilasmos*, meaning the action of propitiation. The foregoing verses clearly tell us that the Lord Jesus Christ offered Himself to God as a propitiatory sacrifice for our sins. He Himself is also the place of propitiation where we are brought back to God and are reconciled to Him.

B. Reconciliation Including Propitiation

Propitiation deals with sins (1 John 2:2; 4:10); reconciliation deals with enmity (2 Cor. 5:19; Rom. 5:10) as well as sins. Therefore, reconciliation includes propitiation. Sinners need propitiation; enemies need reconciliation. Enmity is the greatest problem between man and God. The problem of man being an enemy of God and therefore needing reconciliation is even more serious than the problem of man having sins and therefore needing propitiation. When we were enemies of God, we needed not only propitiation but also reconciliation. Romans 5:10 and 2 Corinthians 5:19 show us that we were not only sinners but also enemies of God. Hence, we needed to be reconciled to God through Christ, through His death with the shedding of His blood, that we might have peace toward God, boast in God, and be saved in life.

SUMMARY

Because of the fall, man is at enmity with God in his mind, disapproves of holding God in his knowledge, hates God, and blasphemes God; he is also a son of disobedience, a child of wrath, and an enemy of God. Therefore, man needs to have a thorough change toward God and be reconciled to Him. However, man does not have the thought of being reconciled to God. Rather, it is God who loves man, delights in man, and desires that man would be reconciled to Him, and who also accomplished a way of propitiation for man. God accomplished reconciliation in Christ, that is, through Christ, and through the death of

Christ with the shedding of His blood, which accomplished redemption, that man may be reconciled to Him. God not only accomplished all the necessary steps of reconciliation through Christ, but He also has given to men the ministry of reconciling people to Him, so that they may become ambassadors of Christ, commissioned to represent Him and to beseech people to be reconciled to God. As a result of our reconciliation to God, we have peace with God and walk toward God on the way of peace; we boast, exult, and glory in God; and we are being saved in life, freed from sins, from the world, from our natural being, from being individualistic, and from other negative things. Reconciliation also includes propitiation. Propitiation deals with sins; reconciliation deals with enmity as well as sins. Formerly, we were not only sinners but also enemies of God. Hence, we needed propitiation and also reconciliation to God.

QUESTIONS

1. Why does man need to be reconciled to God?

2. How did God accomplish the reconciliation of man to Himself?

3. Briefly state the results of reconciliation to God.

4. Briefly explain the relationship between reconciliation and propitiation.

MADE A NEW CREATION

(1)

BEING REGENERATED

OUTLINE

I. The need for regeneration:
   A. Man being of the flesh.
   B. For the entrance into the kingdom of God.

II. The meaning of regeneration:
   A. To be born of God.
   B. To be born from above.
   C. To be born of water and the Spirit.
   D. The Spirit begetting spirit.

III. The accomplishment of regeneration:
   A. According to the purpose and mercy of God the Father.
   B. Through the resurrection of Christ from among the dead.
   C. Through the work of the Holy Spirit.
   D. Through the word of God.
   E. By man's believing.

IV. The results of being regenerated:
   A. Receiving the eternal life of God.
   B. Becoming the children of God.
   C. Becoming the firstfruit of God's new creation.
   D. Obtaining a living hope.

TEXT

In the initial stage of God's full salvation the believers experience God's calling, the Spirit's sanctification, and their repentance, believing, being baptized, being joined to the Triune God, and being redeemed. In the same stage the believers also experience their being regenerated, receiving the Holy Spirit, obtaining the eternal life, being renewed, being transferred, being freed, and thereby being made a new creation (2 Cor. 5:17). The believers' being made a new creation is the most crucial part, even the lifeline, of God's full salvation. The believers are made a new creation first through regeneration. God's redemption, including the forgiveness of sins, washing, sanctification, justification, and reconciliation to God, is for the regeneration of the believers. The reason God forgives us, washes us, sanctifies us, justifies us, and reconciles us to Himself is that we may be regenerated. Our concept might have been that as long as we could be forgiven of our sins and be justified before God, we would have no problems. However, what God's salvation has accomplished includes much more than this. Through God's salvation we not only obtain an outward position that is acceptable to God, but we also are regenerated within to receive a life that is pleasing to God.

I. THE NEED FOR REGENERATION

A. Man Being of the Flesh

Man needs regeneration because man is born of the flesh and is of the flesh (John 3:6). Regardless of how we feel about ourselves, in reality we are from the flesh and of the flesh. That which is from the flesh and of the flesh is flesh. The flesh is born in sin (Psa. 51:5) and is from sin; it is sold under sin (Rom. 7:14) and is of sin. In the flesh there is nothing good (Rom. 7:18); there is only wickedness. The flesh is weak and unprofitable in the things of God (Rom. 8:3; John 6:63), and it is desperately wicked (Jer. 17:9) and incurable. Furthermore, the flesh is enmity against God; it is not and cannot be subject to the law of God, and it cannot please God (Rom. 8:7-8). Being estranged from the life of God (Eph. 4:18), the flesh has nothing to do with God. Moreover, the flesh cannot be changed (Jer. 13:23). Regardless of how much it is changed outwardly, its inward nature cannot be changed at all. No matter how it is changed, it is still the flesh. The flesh is the flesh, and it can never be changed to spirit (John 3:6). Only that which is born of the Spirit is spirit, and only it can receive God's life and partake of the divine nature, escaping the corruption which is in the world by lust (2 Pet. 1:4). Therefore, man needs to be regenerated, that is, to be born of the Spirit, to be born of God, who is the Spirit.

Many think that man needs to be regenerated because man is evil. The fact is that man, whether good or evil, is from the flesh and of the flesh; hence, man needs to be regenerated. We need to be regenerated not only because our life is evil, but because our life is the life of the flesh, not the life of God. Even if our life were good, it still would be the human life, not the divine life. Regardless of how good and pure the human life might be, it still is not the divine life that God desires. Hence, man needs to be regenerated that he may receive God's life.

B. For the Entrance into the Kingdom of God

Man needs to be regenerated that he may enter into the kingdom of God. The Lord Jesus said that man must be born anew (John 3:7), for unless a man is born anew, he cannot enter into the kingdom of God (John 3:3, 5). This word reveals that regeneration is the unique entrance into the kingdom of God.

A kingdom is always related to life. The vegetable kingdom is constituted of the vegetable life, and the animal kingdom, of the animal life. If you intend to share in a certain kind of kingdom, you first need the life of that kingdom. Man and God have two entirely different lives and are in two different realms, in two different kingdoms. In order to enter into the kingdom of God, man must have the life of God, and if he has the life of God, spontaneously he can participate in the kingdom of God. However, in order to have the life of God, man needs to be regenerated. Therefore, man must be regenerated that he may have the divine life and enter into the divine kingdom. Because man's life does not correspond to God's nature, it cannot qualify man to enter into God's kingdom. Even if man had not been corrupted, man still would need to be regenerated that he may have God's life and correspond to God's nature. Only then can he enter into the kingdom that matches God's nature, which is the kingdom of God.

II. THE MEANING OF REGENERATION

To be regenerated means to be born anew. This is why Nicodemus thought that a man needed to enter the second time into his mother's womb and be born (John 3:4). He understood correctly the literal sense of the words "born anew," but he appreciated incorrectly the significance of rebirth, or regeneration. To be regenerated is to be born anew, but it does not mean to enter into the mother's womb and be born a second time.

A. To Be Born of God

To be regenerated is to be born not of blood, nor of the will of the flesh, nor of the will of man, but of God (John 1:12-13). Whoever is born of the flesh receives the human life, which is of the flesh; whoever is born of God obtains the divine life, which is of the Spirit. Hence, as the regenerated ones, we have received the divine life in addition to our human life.

B. To Be Born from Above

To be regenerated is to be born from above. John 3:3 says, "Unless a man is born anew, he cannot see the kingdom of God." Here the word "anew" in Greek is the same word as "from above" in John 3:31. Hence, to be born anew also means to be born from above. When we were born the first time of our parents, we were born of the earth, from below, and the human life of the flesh which we received was out of the earth and of the earth. But when we are born the second time of God, that is, when we are born again, we are born from above, from heaven, and the divine life of the Spirit which we receive is from heaven and of heaven. Hence, to be regenerated is to be born from above to receive the heavenly life.

C. To Be Born of Water and the Spirit

To be born anew is to be born of water and the Spirit. In John 3:5 the Lord Jesus said to Nicodemus, "Unless a man is born of water and the Spirit, he cannot enter into the kingdom of God." The Lord's word here concerning being born of water and the Spirit refers to the birth through the water of baptism preached by John the Baptist and through the Holy Spirit given by the Lord.

Water here signifies death and burial for the termination of the repentant people; the Holy Spirit is the Spirit of life and resurrection for the germination of the terminated ones. This water denotes and signifies the all-inclusive death of Christ. The believers have been baptized into this death (Rom. 6:3), burying not only their old man but also their sins, the world, and their past life and history; they have also been separated from the God-rejecting world and from its corruption. The Holy Spirit is the Spirit of Christ, who is also the Spirit of God (Rom. 8:9). To be baptized into the Holy Spirit is to be baptized into the Spirit of Christ, into Christ Himself (Gal. 3:27; Rom. 6:3), into the Triune God (Matt. 28:19), and even into the Body of Christ (1 Cor. 12:13), which is joined to Christ in one spirit (1 Cor. 6:17). Through baptism in water and in the Spirit, the believers in Christ have been regenerated, leaving all the old things of man and entering into the kingdom of God, into the realm of the divine life and the divine ruling (John 3:3), that they may live by God's eternal life in God's eternal kingdom.

D. The Spirit Begetting Spirit

To be born anew is to be born of the Spirit in our spirit. That is, the Holy Spirit regenerates our human spirit with God's divine life. John 3:6 says, "That which is born of the Spirit is spirit." In this verse, the first Spirit is the divine Spirit, the Holy Spirit of God; the second spirit is the human spirit, the regenerated spirit of man. Regeneration is accomplished in the human spirit by the Holy Spirit of God with the divine life, the eternal, uncreated life of God. Hence, when we are regenerated, the divine Spirit dispenses the divine life, the divine element, into our spirit, enlivening it (Col. 2:13) and making it a new spirit (Ezek. 36:26-27a). This new spirit is our regenerated spirit, our spirit which is born of the divine Spirit. Regeneration, therefore, is the Spirit begetting spirit.

III. THE ACCOMPLISHMENT OF REGENERATION

A. According to the Purpose and Mercy of God the Father

Regeneration is accomplished according to the purpose and mercy of God the Father (James 1:18; 1 Pet. 1:3). The Epistle of James tells us that God brought us forth according to His purpose, that we should be a certain firstfruit of His creatures. This is our divine birth, our regeneration. First Peter 1:3 also tells us that God the Father has regenerated us according to His great mercy. Mercy goes farther than grace. Grace is applied only to a worthy situation, but mercy reaches farther than grace, extending even to the unworthy ones. According to man's condition, no one deserves God's grace. Man is in distress and in a pitiful condition; hence, mercy is needed to bridge the gap between God and man. Therefore, as the fallen and undeserving ones, we have been regenerated according to the purpose and mercy of God the Father.

B. Through the Resurrection of Christ from among the Dead

Regeneration is accomplished through the resurrection of Christ from among the dead (1 Pet. 1:3). On the one hand, the death of Christ redeemed us from our sins, and on the other hand, it released His life (John 12:24). Through the resurrection of Christ, His life entered into us to regenerate us. When He was resurrected, we, His believers, were all included in Him. Thus, we were resurrected with Him (Eph. 2:6). In this resurrection, He imparted the divine life into us and enlivened us with the divine life, bringing us into a relationship of life, an organic union, with God, and making us the same as He is in the divine life and nature. This is regeneration. Hence, God the Father has regenerated us through the resurrection of Christ from among the dead.

C. Through the Work of the Holy Spirit

Regeneration is accomplished through the work of the Holy Spirit (John 3:5, 8). Through His resurrection from among the dead, the Lord Jesus accomplished only the objective fact of our regeneration. Not until the Holy Spirit comes to operate in us and applies the objective fact to us do we have the subjective experience of regeneration. When the Holy Spirit comes, He first convicts us concerning sin, concerning righteousness, and concerning judgment (John 16:8). He causes us to see that we are sinful, that the Lord bore our sins for us that we might be justified, and that unless we believe in Him we shall be judged. Therefore, He convicts us of these things and causes us to repent. Immediately following this, He causes us to believe in the gospel and to receive the Lord Jesus and what He has accomplished for us. Thus we are regenerated, having received the life released by Christ through His death and resurrection.

D. Through the Word of God

Regeneration is accomplished through the word of God.

First Peter 1:23 says, "Having been regenerated, not of corruptible seed, but of incorruptible, through the living and abiding word of God." Here we are told that we have been regenerated of incorruptible seed. A seed is a container of life. The word of God as the incorruptible seed contains God's life. Just as God's life is living and abiding, so the word of God is also living and abiding. Through His living and abiding word of life, God conveys His life into our spirit for our regeneration.

E. By Man's Believing

After the accomplishment of the fact of regeneration by the Lord Jesus through His resurrection from among the dead, and after the operating work of the Holy Spirit, there is still the need of man's believing (John 1:12-13; 3:15) that regeneration may actually take place. Although the Lord has accomplished the fact of regeneration and the Holy Spirit is also moving and working, unless a person believes, he cannot be regenerated. In order to be regenerated, a person needs to believe, and he needs only to believe and not to do anything else. When a person believes into the name of the Lord and receives the Lord as his Savior, he is regenerated, that is, he is born of God and receives God's life with the authority to be a child of God.

IV. THE RESULTS OF BEING REGENERATED

A. Receiving the Eternal Life of God

The first result of our being regenerated is that we receive the life of God (John 3:15-16; 1 John 5:11-13). Since regeneration is the impartation of God's eternal life into our spirit by the divine Spirit, the first and primary thing we receive through regeneration is, of course, the eternal life of God.

The eternal life of God is the contents of God, even God Himself. All that God is and all that is in God are in the life of God. God's nature and all of the divine capabilities and functions in God are contained within this life.

Therefore, when we receive God's eternal life, we receive all that God is in Himself and all that is in God, and we have God's nature and the capabilities and function in God Himself. Hence, we can be as God is and do what God does, that is, we can be like God and live God out.

B. Becoming the Children of God

By being regenerated we have become the children of God (John 1:12-13). Since to be regenerated is to be born of God and to obtain God's life, regeneration automatically causes us to become the children of God, bringing us into a relationship with God in life and nature. The life we receive from God through regeneration enables us to become the children of God, and this life is also our authority to be His children. As God's children, who have God's life and nature, we can be like God, live God, and express God, thus fulfilling the purpose of God's creation of man.

C. Becoming the Firstfruit of God's New Creation

We have been regenerated to become the firstfruit of God's new creation among His creatures. James 1:18 tells us that God has regenerated us by the word of truth according to His own purpose. The word of truth is the word of the divine reality, of what the Triune God is (John 1:14, 17), which word is the seed of life (1 Pet. 1:23). Through this seed of life, God's word of life, God imparts the divine life into us, regenerating us to be the firstfruit of the new creation to participate in His new creation (2 Cor. 5:17), that we may be filled with the vigorous life that matures first for the realization of His eternal purpose.

D. Obtaining a Living Hope

We have been regenerated unto a living hope (1 Pet. 1:3). Through regeneration God enlivens us with His life, bringing us into a relationship of life and nature, an organic union, with Him. Hence, regeneration issues and results in a living hope, a hope of life. This hope in our pilgrimage today is for the future. It is not a hope of objective things, but a hope of life, even the eternal life, with all the endless divine blessings. Formerly, in Adam we all were dead. Our destination was the tomb, and our destiny was death. We were born to die. Everything related to us, in particular, any expectation for the future, was dead. Furthermore, we had no hope and were without God in the world. But because of His mercy, God has regenerated us through the resurrection of Christ, so that we all have been made alive in Christ unto the hope of life. Now the resurrected Christ has become our life within to completely swallow up death, that every aspect of our being may become living and every part may be "lifted." Thus, we have the hope that everything related to us will be living and will be "lifted." Regeneration therefore results in a living hope, a hope of life.

The living hope, the hope of life, which is brought to the regenerated believers through regeneration, may be likened to the various expectations for the future brought to the parents through the birth of a newborn babe. Expectations such as the child's growing up, obtaining an education, entering into a career, getting married, and raising a family all are hinged on the life of the newborn child. Likewise, the life which we have received through regeneration also enables us to have a hope with numerous aspects for this age, for the coming age, and for eternity. In this age we have the hope of growing in life, of maturing, of manifesting our gifts, of exercising our functions, of being transformed, of overcoming, of being redeemed in our body, and of entering into glory. In the coming age we have the hope of entering into the kingdom, of reigning with the Lord, and of enjoying the blessings of the eternal life in the reality of the kingdom of the heavens. In eternity we have the hope of being in the New Jerusalem for the full participation in the consummated blessings of the eternal life in its ultimate manifestation in eternity. This living hope, the hope of life, is hinged on the eternal life which we have received through regeneration. Only this divine life can enable us to grow in life until we enter into the reality of the hope to which we were brought. Thus we will obtain the various blessings mentioned earlier as our inheritance, an inheritance which is incorruptible, unde-filed, and unfading, kept for eternity (1 Pet. 1:3-4).

SUMMARY

Through God's salvation we not only obtain an outward position that is acceptable to God, but we also are regenerated within to receive a life that is pleasing to God and to become His new creation. Man needs regeneration because man is born of the flesh and is of the flesh, which is desperately wicked, incurable, and unchangeable. Even if man had not been corrupted, the life that he possesses still is not the divine life that God desires. Therefore, man must be regenerated to receive the divine life. Only then can he correspond to God's nature and enter into the kingdom that matches God's nature, that is, the kingdom of God. To be regenerated is to be born of God to receive the divine life in addition to our human life, to be born from above to receive the heavenly life of God, and to be born of water and the Spirit, that the believers may leave all the old things and enter into the kingdom of God to live by God's eternal life in God's eternal kingdom. To be regenerated is also to be begotten of the Spirit in our spirit, that is, to be regenerated in our human spirit by the Holy Spirit with the divine life. Regeneration is accomplished in us according to God's purpose and mercy, through the resurrection of Christ from among the dead, through the work of the Holy Spirit, which causes man to repent and believe, and by God's living and abiding word of life. Regeneration first results in our receiving the eternal life of God and participating in all that God is, in all that is in God, in God's nature, and in God's capabilities and functions. Hence, we can be as He is and do what He does, that is, we can be like Him and live Him out. Furthermore, regeneration causes us to have the authority to be the children of God, and it also enables us to become the firstfruit of His new creation, full of the vigorous life that matures first. Finally, regeneration issues in a living hope, even the eternal life, with all the endless divine blessings. This hope is a hope with many aspects for this age, for the coming age, and for eternity. It includes the hope of growing in life, of maturing, of entering into glory, of reigning with the Lord, and of participating fully in the consummated blessings of the eternal life in its ultimate manifestation in eternity, which blessings will be an inheritance, incorruptible, undefiled, and unfading, kept for eternity for us.

QUESTIONS

1. Why does man need regeneration?

2. Briefly explain the meaning of regeneration.

3. How did God regenerate us through the resurrection of Christ from among the dead?

4. How did God regenerate us through the work of the Holy Spirit?

5. What are the results of the believers' being regenerated?

MADE A NEW CREATION

(2)

RECEIVING THE HOLY SPIRIT AND HAVING THE ETERNAL LIFE

OUTLINE

I. Receiving the Holy Spirit:
   A. As the essential Spirit.
   B. As the Spirit of life.
   C. As the seal.
   D. As the pledge.
   E. As the indwelling Spirit.
   F. As the reality of Christ.

II. Having the eternal life:
   A. The life of God:
      1. From the beginning.
      2. With the Father.
      3. Manifested to the apostles.
   B. The life in the Son of God.
   C. The free gift of God in Christ.
   D. Received by faith.
   E. Assured by the Word of God.
   F. Those having eternal life to by no means perish forever.

TEXT

In the initial stage of God's full salvation, the stage of regeneration, the believers are made a new creation by being regenerated, by receiving the Holy Spirit, and by having the eternal life of God. Since we have covered the matter of regeneration, we shall proceed to see the matters of receiving the Holy Spirit and having the eternal life.

I. RECEIVING THE HOLY SPIRIT

We receive the Spirit through hearing and believing the gospel (Gal. 3:2). When we hear the word of the truth, the gospel of our salvation, the Holy Spirit begins to move within us, urging us to believe in and receive Christ. When we believe in and receive Christ, we are regenerated. At this time, on the one hand, God causes His Spirit to impart His life into our spirit to enliven our dead spirit; on the other hand, He puts His Spirit into our spirit, that is, He causes His Spirit to dwell in our enlivened new spirit. Hence, we, the regenerated ones, not only have obtained the eternal life of God but also have received the Spirit to indwell us.

According to the revelation of the Bible, the indwelling Spirit in us has the following six main functions:

A. As the Essential Spirit

First, the Spirit enters into us as the essential Spirit for our existence, being, life, and living. He is the ultimate consummation of the processed Triune God, the life-giving Spirit whom Christ became in resurrection (1 Cor. 15:45). This Spirit enters into us who have believed in Christ (John 20:22) and lives in us to be the essence of the divine life, nature, and being within us.

B. As the Spirit of Life

The Spirit enters into us as the Spirit of life (Rom. 8:2). Life is the contents of the divine Trinity. When the Spirit of life enters into us, He imparts the eternal life of God into us to be our life. According to the revelation of Romans chapter eight, the Spirit of life is the Spirit of God, the Spirit of Christ, and even Christ Himself (vv. 9-10). First, the Spirit of life comes into our spirit to make our spirit life (v. 10). Then He spreads from our spirit into our mind to make our mind a mind of life (v. 6). Finally, He imparts this life even into our mortal bodies to make the body of death a body of life (v. 11). Thus the Spirit of life fills our entire being, including our spirit, soul, and body, sanctifying us and conforming us to the image of the firstborn Son of God (v. 29) that we may become the many sons of God to be His corporate expression.

C. As the Seal

The Holy Spirit enters into us also as the seal within us (Eph. 1:13; 4:30; 2 Cor. 1:22). A seal is a mark. That we, the believers, are sealed with the Holy Spirit means that we are marked with the Holy Spirit as a living seal, indicating that we belong to God, that is, that we are God's inheritance (Eph. 1:11). Furthermore, a seal also has an image. When we are sealed with the Holy Spirit, we bear the image of God signified by the seal. Thus we are made like God and can express God.

The Holy Spirit is the seal and also the sealing within us. The Spirit as the seal comes into us once for all, but the sealing of the Spirit continues until every part of our being is sealed, even unto the redemption, the transfiguration, of our body. As Ephesians 1:13 and 14 tell us, we were sealed with the Holy Spirit unto the redemption of God's acquired possession. At the time of our regeneration, the Spirit as the seal was put into our spirit, and His sealing began within us. This sealing is spreading from our spirit to our mind, emotion, and will for the sanctification and transformation of our soul. Eventually, even our body will be thoroughly sealed, that is, saturated and transfigured; that will be the redemption of our body.

D. As the Pledge

The Holy Spirit is not only the seal within us but also the pledge of the divine inheritance (Eph. 1:14; 2 Cor. 1:22b; 5:5b). In God's economy we are an inheritance to God (Eph. 1:11), and God is an inheritance to us (Eph. 1:14). God and we are a mutual inheritance. For us to be God's inheritance, the sealing of the Holy Spirit is needed; for God to be our inheritance, the pledging of the Holy Spirit is required. The Greek word for pledge also means foretaste, guarantee. As the pledge of our inheritance, the Spirit is not only a guarantee, assuring us that all that God is and all that God has shall be our inheritance, but He is also a foretaste of what we shall inherit of all that God is to us.

Therefore, as the seal, the Holy Spirit forms the divine elements into an impression in us for God's expression; as the pledge, He gives us a foretaste as a sample and guarantee of the full taste of God.

E. As the Indwelling Spirit

The Holy Spirit in us is also the indwelling Spirit (Rom. 8:9; 1 Cor. 6:19). In John 14:17 the Lord Jesus clearly and definitely promised that when the Holy Spirit came He would indwell the disciples. Then on the night of His resurrection, He came into the midst of the disciples and breathed into them that they might receive the Holy Spirit (John 20:22). That was the fulfillment of the promise of the Spirit's indwelling the disciples. In the Epistles, Paul also stressed the Spirit's indwelling. Romans 8:9 says that "the Spirit of God dwells in you," and verse 11 refers to "His Spirit who indwells you." The word dwell in Greek means "to make home." The Spirit of God comes into us not only to be the seal and the pledge, the guarantee, the foretaste, but even more to dwell in us, to make His home in us. This is a particular blessing given by God to us in the New Testament age; it was not there in the Old Testament times. In the Old Testament age, God caused His Spirit to come and work only upon man outwardly; He did not cause

His Spirit to dwell in man. Not until after Christ's death
and resurrection did God Himself as the consummated
Spirit enter into the believers to be the indwelling Spirit.
He comes into us not to visit but to settle down in us, to
make His home in us, even to occupy our whole being, that
He may reveal God and Christ to us and that we may
receive and enjoy all the riches of God in Christ.

F. As the Reality of Christ

The indwelling Spirit in us is also the reality of Christ.
John 14:16-20 reveals that the Comforter who was coming
was the embodiment of Christ. Verse 17 says that "the
Spirit of reality...abides with you," and verse 18 says, "I
[Christ] am coming to you." Again, verse 17 says that "He
[the Holy Spirit]...shall be in you," and verse 20 says, "I
[Christ] in you." This clearly indicates that when the Spirit
comes, it is Christ who comes, and that when the Spirit is
in us, it is Christ who is in us. The Spirit is Christ, and
Christ is the Spirit. The Spirit who indwells us is the
Christ who died and was resurrected and who indwells us.

John 14:26 says, "But the Comforter, the Holy Spirit,
whom the Father will send in My name..." The Comforter
is the Holy Spirit, whom the Father will send in the name
of the Son. To come in the name of the Son is to come as
the Son. This proves that when the Spirit comes, it is the
Son who comes, and that when the Spirit dwells in us, it is
Christ the Son who dwells in us.

John 16:12-15 further indicates that the Spirit's indwelling the believers is to reveal Christ, to glorify Christ, and
to make Christ real in the believers. Verse 13 says, "But
when He, the Spirit of reality, comes, He will guide you
into all the reality." The Spirit of reality does not guide the
believers into the doctrine concerning Christ but into all
the reality of Christ, so that all that Christ is and has may
become real to the believers. All that God is and has is
embodied in Christ (Col. 2:9; John 16:15), and all that Christ
is and has is received by the Spirit and is revealed to the

believers through the Spirit (John 16:14, 15). Therefore, when the Spirit is in us, it is Christ who is in us. The Spirit is not Christ's representative in us, but Christ's reality.

For example, the Bible says that God is light (1 John 1:5), and it also says that Christ is light (John 8:12). This light can be realized in us only through the Spirit. When the Spirit moves within us, the light shines. The light is both the Father and the Son. The Father is the source and the essence of light, and the Son is the embodiment and expression of this light. We realize this light in actuality through the Spirit. When the Spirit moves within us, He is the reality of light.

The same is true with the matter of life. The Father is the source and the essence of life, and the Son is the embodiment and expression of this life. Through the Spirit this life becomes our experience and enjoyment. Romans 8:2 says that the Spirit is the Spirit of life. When the Spirit moves within us, He is the reality of life. He is not only the shining and enlightening light but also the very life which enlivens, nourishes, and strengthens us.

II. HAVING THE ETERNAL LIFE

The Bible shows us that the matter of having the eternal life and enjoying the blessing of the eternal life is divided into three different periods—having eternal life in the present age, having eternal life in the coming age, and enjoying eternal life in the eternal age. In this lesson we shall cover only the matter of having eternal life in the present age.

We receive eternal life in the present age at the time of our believing. When we believe into Christ, we receive eternal life in this age; we do not have to wait until the coming age or the eternal age.

A. The Life of God

The eternal life is the life of God. The Greek word for this life is *zoe*, denoting the divine spiritual life; it is not *psuche*, denoting the human soulish life, nor *bios*, denoting the physical life. In the Bible, the word "eternal" denotes not only duration of time, which is everlasting, without beginning or end, but also the quality, which is absolutely perfect and complete, without any shortage or defect. In the whole universe, besides the life of God, there is no other life that has this nature. God is eternal, without beginning or end, and He is absolutely perfect and complete. Therefore, His life is also eternal, without beginning or end, and it is absolutely perfect and complete. This life of God, which is without beginning or end and which is also absolutely perfect and complete, is the eternal life.

1. From the Beginning

The eternal life is the life which was from the beginning (1 John 1:1). It was already there at the beginning of creation; that is, it preceded the universe and time. This indicates that this life is uncreated, without beginning or end, self-existing, ever-existing, and never changing. In the universe, God alone is uncreated; He is from everlasting to everlasting (Psa. 90:2), without beginning or end, self-existing and ever-existing (Exo. 3:14), and never changing (Psa. 102:27). Since God Himself is such, the life which is God Himself must also be such. Therefore, the divine life is the eternal life, and the eternal life is the divine life, the life which was from the beginning.

2. With the Father

The eternal life is the life which was with the Father (1 John 1:2). The phrase "with the Father" in 1 John 1:2 indicates that the Father is the source of the eternal life and that the eternal life and the Father are one.

3. Manifested to the Apostles

The eternal life is the life which was manifested to the apostles (1 John 1:2). This life which was manifested to the apostles is the Son who was with the Father and who was manifested with the Father as the expression of the eternal life. The apostles saw this life and then testified and reported this life to the believers. What they reported was not some theology or doctrine but the divine, eternal life, which they saw and testified by their practical experiences. The manifestation of the eternal life is for the purpose of revealing and imparting life to men, so that those whom the Father has chosen may partake of and enjoy this life and may be brought into the union and communion of this life with the Father.

B. The Life in the Son of God

Eternal life is the life which is in the Son of God (John 1:4). The Son of God is the expression of God, and God Himself is hidden in His Son. Hence, the life of God is in His Son. This life which is in the Son of God is the eternal life. Therefore, he who has the Son of God has the life, and he who does not have the Son of God does not have the life (1 John 5:11-12). When we receive the Son of God, we have the eternal life, which is in Him.

C. The Free Gift of God in Christ

Eternal life is the free gift of God in Christ. Romans 6:23 says that "the free gift of God is eternal life in Christ Jesus our Lord." First John 5:11 also says that "God gave to us eternal life." These two verses clearly indicate that God has given to us His life, the eternal life, as a free gift in Christ. There is no need for us to pay any price for it; we simply need to receive it and we have it.

D. Received by Faith

Man receives eternal life by faith. Because God loved us, He put His life, the eternal life, in His Son and gave His life to us that we might receive it. The way to receive this life is to believe in His Son. When we receive the Son by believing in Him, we shall not perish, but have eternal life (John 3:16). Since God has put His life, the eternal life, in

His Son and has given it to us as a gift, when we receive the Son by believing in Him, spontaneously we have the eternal life which is in the Son (John 3:36; 6:47).

Therefore, as soon as we hear the gospel and believe into Christ, we have eternal life (John 5:24). Many people think that after we believe in the Lord today, we must wait until the future to have eternal life. The fact is that there is no space of time between "believing" and "having." When we believe in the Lord, immediately we have eternal life (1 John 5:12); we do not need to wait even for one moment, much less until the future.

E. Assured by the Word of God

That we have eternal life is assured by the Word of God. First John 5:13 says, "I write these things to you that you may know that you have eternal life, to you who believe in the name of the Son of God." This verse indicates that the written words of the Scriptures are the assurance to the believers, who believe into the name of the Son of God, that they have eternal life. Our believing to receive eternal life is the fact; the words of the holy writings are the assurance concerning this fact. We are assured and have the pledge by these words that because we believe into the name of the Son of God we have eternal life, and we know that we have it now.

F. Those Having Eternal Life to by No Means Perish Forever

Since we have eternal life, we shall by no means perish forever. John 10:28-29 says, "And I give to them eternal life, and they shall by no means perish forever, and no one shall snatch them out of My hand. My Father who has given them to Me is greater than all, and no one can snatch them out of My Father's hand."

Since the life which we have received is the eternal life, we shall never perish. Because of the eternal nature of this life, we shall live forever and not perish. Furthermore, we

who have eternal life are also in the hands of the Lord and
the Father. Both the Lord's hand as the hand of power and
the Father's hand as the hand of love are for the believers'
protection. Eternal life shall never run out, and the hands
of the Son and the Father shall never fail. Hence, the
believers are eternally secure and shall never perish.

SUMMARY

When we are regenerated by hearing the word of the
truth and by believing in Christ, we receive the Holy Spirit
from God and we also have the eternal life of God. When
we receive the Holy Spirit, we receive Him as the essential
Spirit for our existence, being, life, and living. As the Spirit
of life, He continually imparts God's eternal life to us until
our entire being is filled with Him. As the seal, He marks
us out, indicating that we are God's inheritance, and He
also impresses us with the image of God that we may be
made like God to express Him. As the pledge, He assures
us that all that God is and all that God has shall be our
inheritance, and He also gives us a foretaste of what we
shall inherit of all that God is to us. As the indwelling
Spirit, He is settling down in us, making His home in us,
and even occupying our whole being. As the reality of
Christ, He brings us into all the reality of Christ so that all
that Christ is and has may become real in us.

When we receive eternal life, we receive the life of God.
Eternal life is without beginning or end, and it is also
absolutely perfect and complete. It is the life which was
from the beginning and which was with the Father and
one with the Father. In time it was manifested to the

apostles for the purpose of revealing and imparting life to men, so that those whom the Father has chosen may partake of and enjoy it. Furthermore, it is the life that is in the Son of God, and it is the free gift of God in Christ. We need only to believe into Christ, and immediately we have eternal life. This is a fact assured by the Word of God. Moreover, because of the eternal nature of this life, we shall live and shall by no means perish forever. Not only so, we are also in the hands of the Lord and the Father. Eternal life shall never run out, and the hands of the Son and the Father shall never fail. Hence, we are eternally secure and shall never perish.

QUESTIONS

1. What are the six main functions of the Holy Spirit who dwells in the believers?

2. What are the issues of the Spirit's being the Spirit of life in the believers?

3. Briefly explain the function of the Spirit as the seal and the pledge in the believers.

4. Briefly explain the Spirit's being the reality of Christ in the believers.

5. The matter of having the eternal life is divided into which three periods?

6. Briefly explain the fact that the eternal life is the life of God.

7. Use the Scriptures to prove that the eternal life is the gift of God received by man as soon as he believes in the Lord.

LESSON FORTY-THREE

MADE A NEW CREATION

(3)

BEING RENEWED

OUTLINE

I. The need for renewing.

II. The accomplishment of renewing:
A. By the Holy Spirit.
B. Through the washing of regeneration.

III. The results of being renewed:
A. Becoming a new creation.
B. Becoming heirs.
C. Becoming the new man:
1. Through the cross of Christ:
a. Terminating the old creation.
b. Abolishing the ordinances.
2. Being created into one new man:
a. In Christ.
b. With Christ as the essence.

TEXT

In the initial stage of God's full salvation, the stage of regeneration, the believers are made a new creation by being regenerated, by receiving the Holy Spirit, by having God's eternal life, and by being renewed.

I. THE NEED FOR RENEWING

When man was first created. he was not crooked, wicked, or unclean, but upright, good, and clean (Eccl. 7:29). At that time man was without sin, corruption, or defect; therefore, in the eyes of God man was very good (Gen. 1:31). However, through the fall Satan entered into man with the satanic life (John 8:44; 1 John 3:10), man became mixed and unclean, and he also became the old man. Furthermore, sin (Rom. 7:23) and lust were constituted into the human body, because Satan's life, the poisonous element of sin, was mixed into it; therefore, the human body was transmuted and became flesh (Gen. 3:7). Thus, man became the Devil's possession (1 John 3:8), being obedient to the evil spirits (Eph. 2:2). Not only so, man is also brought forth in iniquity (Psa. 51:5), his heart is deceitful above all things and desperately wicked (Jer. 17:9), and nothing good dwells in his flesh, which is filled with all kinds of wicked things (Rom. 7:18; Mark 7:20-23). Moreover, he is at enmity with God, not subject to the law of God, nor can he be, and he cannot please God (Rom. 8:7-8). Therefore, man needs to be renewed. Only through renewing can God dispense the divine essence of the new creation into man, that man may pass from his old state into a wholly new one, from the old creation into the status of a new creation.

II. THE ACCOMPLISHMENT OF RENEWING

A. By the Holy Spirit

All the work of renewing that God does in us is carried out by the Holy Spirit (Titus 3:5). The work of the Holy

Spirit within us begins with regeneration and continues with renewing. The Holy Spirit renews us by imparting the divine essence into our being that we may become a new creation. He is the divine Person, the ultimate consummation of the processed Triune God who has passed through incarnation, human living, crucifixion, resurrection, and ascension. He washes and renews us with the divine essence that we may become a new creation, having the divine life and nature, and may be heirs of God in His eternal life, inheriting all the riches of the Triune God. Therefore, renewing is carried out by the Holy Spirit.

B. Through the Washing of Regeneration

God does the renewing work in us through the washing of regeneration (Titus 3:5). The washing of regeneration is the process of God's new creation to make us a new man. It is a reconditioning, remaking, or remodeling, with life. This washing of regeneration begins with our being born again and continues with the renewing of the Holy Spirit. The washing of regeneration begins in us at the time of our regeneration, through which we obtain from God His life and nature. This divine life and nature cause us to be delivered from our natural life and nature, which through the fall have become defiled. Thus, when we are delivered from our natural life and nature through God's divine life and nature, we are cleansed from all defilement. This purging is carried out through the washing of regeneration at the time of our new birth. Immediately following this, the Holy Spirit continues to do the work of renewing within us, imparting into us the divine essence of the new creation. The divine elements of the new creation produce in us a metabolic change that causes the old and natural elements within us to be replaced. This is the continuing work carried out by the washing of regeneration together with the renewing of the Holy Spirit. Both the washing of regeneration and the renewing of the Holy Spirit are a continual working in us throughout our whole life until the completion of the new creation.

III. THE RESULTS OF BEING RENEWED

A. Becoming a New Creation

Since by being renewed we have received the divine essence of the new creation, we are made a new creation. This new creation is in contrast to the old creation (2 Cor. 5:17). The old creation is our old man in Adam (Eph. 4:22), our natural being by birth, without the divine life and nature; the new creation is the new man in Christ (Eph. 4:24), our being which is regenerated by the Spirit (John 3:6), having God's life and the divine nature (John 3:16; 2 Pet. 1:4), with Christ as its constituents (Col. 3:10-11). It is this new creation that fulfills God's eternal purpose by expressing God in the divine sonship. This is the result of God's renewing work in the believers through the Holy Spirit.

B. Becoming Heirs

Since we are renewed through regeneration to receive the divine essence, we are also made heirs of God, who are qualified to inherit the estate of God the Father (Rom. 4:14; 8:17; Gal. 3:29; 4:7), according to the hope of eternal life (Titus 3:7). This eternal life, which is our enjoyment in this age and our hope in the coming age, is not only for us to live and enjoy God in this age, but also for us to inherit all the riches of what God is to us in the coming age and in eternity. Hence, we have the hope of eternal life. According to this hope we are made heirs of God to inherit all His riches for eternity. This also is an issue of our being renewed by the Holy Spirit.

C. Becoming the New Man

As a result of our being renewed, we are made a new creation, which is the new man in Christ (Eph. 2:15; 4:24; Col. 3:10). This new man was created by Christ, who through the cross abolished in His flesh the law of commandments in ordinances and broke down the middle wall of partition, thus creating the Jewish believers and the Gentile believers in Himself into the new man.

1. Through the Cross of Christ

In order to create in Himself one new man, Christ terminated the entire old creation on the cross and abolished the separating ordinances that caused enmity between peoples.

a. Terminating the Old Creation

As the Firstborn of all creation (Col. 1:15), Christ died on the cross in the old creation, thus terminating the entire old creation. When Christ was crucified in His flesh on the cross, the entire old creation was included in Him. According to Hebrews 10:20, the veil in the temple typifies the flesh of Christ. On the veil cherubim were embroidered, signifying all the creatures. When Christ was crucified on the cross, the veil in the temple was rent from top to bottom (Matt. 27:51), and the cherubim on it also were rent. This shows that when Christ's flesh died on the cross, all the creatures also were crucified together with this flesh. Therefore, the death of Christ not only dealt with sin and the flesh, destroyed Satan and the world belonging to him, and terminated the old man, but it also ended the entire old creation.

b. Abolishing the Ordinances

The death of Christ abolished the separating ordinances that cause enmity between peoples. On the cross Christ abolished in His flesh the law of the commandments in ordinances (Eph. 2:15). The law of the commandments in ordinances does not refer to the law of moral commandments but to the law of the ritual commandments, such as the ordinances of circumcision, keeping the Sabbath, and eating certain foods. These ordinances were given by God to the Jews because of man's flesh. The principal one among them is circumcision, which is for the cutting off of man's flesh. In addition, the Jews were required to keep the Sabbath and to observe many regulations concerning their diet. This created a great distinction and separation between the Jews and the Gentiles, which became the cause of enmity between them (Eph. 2:14). Therefore, in order to produce the new man, Christ needed to break down the middle wall of partition between the Jews and the Gentiles by abolishing the law of the commandments in ordinances and thus removing the enmity between them.

It was in His flesh that Christ abolished the law of the commandments in ordinances. While Christ was in His flesh on the cross, all the ordinances also were nailed with Him to the cross (Col. 2:14). Through this, Christ abolished in His flesh the law of the commandments in ordinances, broke down the middle wall of partition, slew the enmity between the Jews and the Gentiles, and created the two in Himself into one new man.

2. Being Created into One New Man

a. In Christ

The new man was created in Christ Himself (Eph. 2:15). Christ is the sphere and the means in and by which the new man was created. Apart from being in Him, we could not have been created into one new man. Christ died in His flesh, abolishing the law of the commandments in ordinances and terminating all the negative things; then in resurrection He became the wonderful Spirit (1 Cor. 15:45b). It is in this wonderful Spirit, who is the resurrected Christ Himself, that we have been created into one new man. Therefore, the new man was created in Christ Himself.

b. With Christ as the Essence

This phrase "in Himself" (Eph. 2:15) indicates that

Christ was not only the Creator of the new man, but also the sphere in which, the means by which, and the essence with which the new man was created. With Himself as the essence and in Himself, He created the Jews and the Gentiles into one new man. Therefore, Christ is the essence of the new man. Through Christ's being the essence of the new man, God's divine nature has been wrought into humanity. In the old creation God did not work His nature into any of His creatures, not even into man. In the creation of the one new man, however, God's nature has been wrought into man to make His divine nature one entity with humanity. Christ then became the essence of this entity—the new man. This also is the result of God's renewing work in us.

SUMMARY

Through renewing God dispenses the divine essence of the new creation into man, that man may pass from his old state into a wholly new one, from the old creation into the status of a new creation. Man needs to be renewed not only because he has become the old man and the flesh through his fall and corruption, but also because he does not have God's essence in him. All the work of renewing that God does in us is carried out by the Holy Spirit. The Holy Spirit imparts God's essence into our being that we may become the new creation with God's life and nature. Furthermore, God renews us through the washing of regeneration. This washing of regeneration begins with our being born again and, together with the renewing of the Holy Spirit, continues to work in us, purging away all the old and natural elements. As a result of being renewed, we are made a new creation, which is the new man in Christ, having God's life and nature and with Christ as its constituents, that we may become heirs of God, who are qualified to inherit all the estate of God the Father, according to the hope of eternal life. Moreover, by abolishing in His flesh the law of the commandments in ordinances, Christ created the Jewish believers and the Gentile believers in Himself into one new man, and He also became the essence of this new man.

QUESTIONS

1. Why does man need to be renewed?

2. What is the washing of regeneration?

3. How does the Holy Spirt do the work of renewing in us?

4. What is the new creation? How do the believers become the new creation?

5. How was the new man created?

LESSON FORTY-FOUR

MADE A NEW CREATION

(4)

BEING TRANSFERRED

OUTLINE

I. The need of a transfer.

II. The basis of the transfer:
   A. God.
   B. Christ.

III. The results of being transferred:
   A. Out of darkness into light.
   B. From the authority of Satan to God.
   C. Out of the authority of darkness into the kingdom of the Son of God's love.
   D. Out of Adam into Christ.
   E. From law to grace.
   F. Out of the evil age into Christ and the church.

TEXT

When a believer is regenerated, receives the Holy Spirit, obtains God's eternal life, and is renewed by the Holy Spirit, he is transferred out of the authority of the darkness of Satan into the kingdom of the Son of God's love, out of Adam into Christ, from law to grace, and out of the evil and crooked age into Christ and the church.

I. THE NEED OF A TRANSFER

Before they received God's salvation, the believers were in a number of pitiful realms. At that time they were sitting in darkness and in the shadow of death (Luke 1:79). They were under the authority of Satan, being ruled and controlled by him, and they were also lying under his hand, being manipulated and slaughtered by him as he willed (Acts 26:18; 1 John 5:19). Constituted sinners in Adam (Rom. 5:19), they were condemned by God (Rom. 5:18). Being dead (1 Cor. 15:22), they were powerless in doing good and insensitive in committing sins. Under the law they were exposed, condemned (Rom. 3:19; 5:20a), cursed (Gal. 3:10), and enslaved (Gal. 4:7). They were in a crooked and perverted generation (Phil. 2:15) and in an evil religious age (Gal. 1:4; Acts 2:40b), unable to know the grace of the gospel of Christ. Therefore, how much they needed to be transferred out of these pitiful and tragic realms that they might enter into an entirely new sphere.

II. THE BASIS OF THE TRANSFER

A. God

It is of God who calls them that the believers are transferred out of darkness into light (1 Pet. 2:9). God has called and delivered them out of Satan's death-realm of darkness into His life-realm of light. It is also of God that the believers are delivered out of the authority of darkness and are transferred into the kingdom of the Son of His love (Col. 1:13). God has delivered them out of the authority of darkness, the kingdom of Satan, and has transferred them into the kingdom of Christ, the kingdom of the Son of His love, that they may be qualified to partake of Christ as their portion. It is also of God that the believers are no longer in Adam but in Christ, for it is God who has put them in Christ (1 Cor. 1:30a), transferring them out of Adam into Christ. It is of God's eternal will that the believers have been rescued out of the present evil age, the religious age (Gal. 1:4). In His eternal economy God has arranged that Christ should give Himself for man's sins to rescue man out of the present evil age, the religious age, that man may enter into Christ and the church. Therefore, it is of God that the believers have been transferred out of these pitiful and tragic realms.

B. Christ

It is of Christ that the believers have been transferred from darkness to light and from the authority of Satan to God (Acts 26:17-18). As the light of the world (John 8:12), Christ shined on those sitting in darkness and in the shadow of death (Matt. 4:16). He also sent His messengers into the midst of the fallen people, that their eyes might be opened that they might turn from darkness to light and from the authority of Satan to God. It is also of Christ that the believers have been transferred from law to grace. Grace came through Jesus Christ (John 1:17). When Christ came, grace also came. Grace is Christ (compare Gal. 2:20 and 1 Cor. 15:10b), that is, it is God in Christ becoming our life, our life power, and everything for us to enjoy. It is also of Christ that the believers have been delivered out of the religious age, which is evil and crooked, into Christ and the church. Christ gave Himself for man's sins that He might rescue man from the present evil age, that is, the religious world (Gal. 1:4). Moreover, as the good Shepherd, He led out the sheep that were in the fold (denoting the Jewish believers) with the other sheep (denoting the Gentile believers), forming them into one flock (signifying the one church) under one Shepherd, who is Christ Himself (John 10:11, 16). Therefore, it is of Christ that the believers have been transferred out of darkness, out of the authority of Satan, out of the law, and out of the evil, crooked age.

III. THE RESULTS OF BEING TRANSFERRED

A. Out of Darkness into Light

Both Acts 26:18 and 1 Peter 2:9 point out that God has transferred His believers out of darkness into light. Darkness is a sign of sin and death; light is a sign of righteousness and life. Formerly, we were fallen into darkness; we lived, walked, and behaved ourselves in darkness (Matt. 4:16). Because of God's salvation, however, we have been transferred out of darkness into light.

B. From the Authority of Satan to God

As a result of being transferred, the believers have been moved not only out of darkness into light, but even more from the authority of Satan to God (Acts 26:18). In his fall man fell away from the presence of God into the authority of Satan and became a child of the Devil (1 John 3:8a, 10; John 8:44) with the satanic life and nature. Today the whole world lies in the evil one (1 John 5:19), and the people of the world are being manipulated and slaughtered by Satan as he wills. Because of God's deliverance, however, we have been transferred out of the authority of Satan that we may turn to God. Now we are no longer under the power of Satan but under the authority of God.

C. Out of the Authority of Darkness into the Kingdom of the Son of God's Love

As a result of being transferred, the believers also have been delivered out of the authority of darkness into the kingdom of the Son of God's love (Col. 1:13). God is light, and Satan is darkness. Hence, the authority of darkness denotes the authority of Satan. Satan's authority of darkness is the authority of evil in the air, in the heavenlies (Eph. 6:12). Matthew 12:26 indicates that Satan has his kingdom. The authority of evil, of rebellion, in the heavenlies is the kingdom of Satan, the authority of darkness. The kingdom of Satan is a system. Not everything in this system is evil in the eyes of men. On the contrary, many things, such as knowledge and philosophy, are considered good by men. However, after speaking of the authority of darkness in Colossians 1, Paul goes on to mention ordinances, observances, philosophies, and the elements of the world, indicating that they are different aspects of the satanic authority. Satan uses different aspects of his authority to control people, to lord it over them, and to keep them under his rule.

Through the death of Christ on the cross God has dealt with Satan's authority over us by destroying his power, that we may be delivered out of the authority of darkness and be transferred into the kingdom of the Son of His love. The kingdom of God's beloved Son is the authority of Christ (Rev. 11:15; 12:10). The Son of the Father's love is the object of the Father's love to be the embodiment of life to us in the divine love with the authority in resurrection. This is the kingdom of the Son of God's love. When we are transferred into the kingdom of God's beloved Son, we are restricted and ruled in His divine love with the authority in resurrection. In our experience, as we love the Lord Jesus, we are conscious of a sweet sense of love, and we realize that we also are the objects of the divine love. As objects of this divine love, we spontaneously come under a certain control or ruling, no longer free to do whatever we wish according to the desire in our heart. This rule is not harsh; rather, it is sweet and pleasant. We are restricted and ruled in such a sweet way. This is the kingdom of the Son of God's love. Now we have been delivered out of the authority of darkness and transferred into the kingdom of the Son of God's love.

D. Out of Adam into Christ

By being transferred the believers have been moved out of Adam into Christ. In the eyes of God there are only two men on the earth: Adam and Christ. Adam is the first man, and he is also the initial man; Christ is the second Man, and He is also the last Man (1 Cor. 15:45, 47). Originally, we were all in Adam, being constituted sinners (Rom. 5:19), condemned (Rom. 5:18), and dead (1 Cor. 15:22). By His salvation, however, God has transferred us out of Adam into Christ (1 Cor. 1:30). Now in Christ we have been constituted righteous (Rom. 5:19) and justified unto life (Rom. 5:18). In Him we also have received every spiritual blessing given by God (Eph. 1:3), such as being selected, predestinated, and redeemed (Eph. 1:4, 5, 7), receiving the sonship (Eph. 1:5), receiving God as our inheritance (Eph. 1:11, 14), and being raised up together with Christ and seated together with Him in the heavenlies (Eph. 2:6). This is the result of the believers' being transferred out of Adam into Christ.

E. From Law to Grace

As a result of such a transfer, the believers have been transferred from law to grace (Rom. 6:14). Before they believed in the Lord, they were all living under law. The Jews were under the Mosaic law, and the Gentiles were under their self-made law. However, no one in the world, whether Jew or Gentile, is justified before God by law; on the contrary, everyone is bound, condemned, and cursed under law (Rom. 7:6; Gal. 3:10-11).

God's purpose in giving the law through Moses was first to expose man's fallen condition. The law was not in the origination of God's economy. It was added because of man's transgressions while God's economy was proceeding (Gal. 3:19), that all men might have the knowledge of sin, that every mouth might be stopped, and that all the world might become subject to the judgment of God (Rom. 3:19-20). Second, the law was given to guard man unto

Christ. Galatians 3:23 says, "But before faith came we were guarded under law, being shut up unto the faith which was about to be revealed." In God's economy the law was used as a sheepfold to keep God's chosen people until Christ came. Third, the law was given to conduct man to Christ. As a child-conductor, the law brings us to Christ (Gal. 3:24). The law was used by God as a custodian, a guardian, a child-conductor, to watch over His chosen people before Christ came, and to escort and conduct them to Christ at the proper time. Now that Christ has come, we should come to Christ and should be no longer under law.

When Christ came, grace also came (John 1:17), because grace is Christ (compare Gal. 2:20 and 1 Cor. 15:10b). On the one hand, Christ died for us, redeeming us from the condemnation of the law; on the other hand, He brought us together with Him into death that we may be delivered from the bondage of law, and He also raised us up together with Him that we may have His life and live under God's grace. In this grace the processed Triune God has become our life and everything that we may enjoy the Triune God as our life and life supply. This is the result of God's transferring the believers from law to grace.

F. Out of the Evil Age into Christ and the Church

Through such a transfer the believers have been transferred out of the evil and crooked age, that is, the religious age, into Christ and the church. Galatians 1:4 says, "Who [Christ] gave Himself for our sins, that He might rescue us out of the present evil age, according to the will of our God and Father." An age is a part of the world as the satanic system. The present evil age here, according to the context of Galatians, refers to the religious world, the religious course of the world, the Jewish religion. This is confirmed by 6:14-15, where circumcision is considered a part of the world. The purpose of Christ's giving Himself for our sins was to rescue us, to pluck us, out of the Jewish religion, the present evil age. This is to release God's chosen people from the custody of the law, to bring them out of the sheepfold (John 10:1, 3), into the grace of the gospel according to the will of God.

In Acts 2:40 Peter entreated the repenting Jews, saying, "Be saved from this crooked generation." Peter did not say, "Be saved from God's condemnation," or, "Be saved from eternal perdition." Instead, he said, "Be saved from this crooked generation." The phrase "this crooked generation" refers to the perverted Jews in that age who rejected God's Christ (v. 36) and were considered by God as the present evil age. The repenting Jews needed to be saved from that evil age. This indicates that they needed to turn to God not only from their sins but also from their generation, their Jewish society, including their Jewish religion. The result of such a salvation of God is an entrance into a new generation—the church.

John 10 also reveals to us that Christ, as the good Shepherd, entered into the sheepfold to lead His sheep out of the fold and to bring them into the pasture. The sheepfold signifies the law, or Judaism as the religion of the law. Before Christ came, God used Judaism as a sheepfold to keep His sheep. When Christ came, He led His sheep out of the fold into the pasture, that they might feast on His riches. In verse 16 the Lord also said, "I have other sheep which are not of this fold; I must bring them also...and there shall be one flock, one shepherd." "Other sheep" refer to the Gentile believers. "One flock" refers to the one church, the one Body of Christ, including the believing Jews and Gentiles. Christ brings both together into one flock and under one Shepherd. This indicates that He delivers the Jewish and Gentile believers out of the religious fold, the religious world, and transfers them into Christ and the church.

SUMMARY

Before receiving God's salvation, man was in darkness, under the authority of Satan, in Adam, under law, and in the crooked, perverted age and the evil, religious age. Hence, man was in a number of pitiful and tragic conditions. By the salvation of God the Father and the Lord Jesus Christ, however, we have been transferred out of those different conditions into an entirely new sphere. As a result of being transferred, we have been moved out of the realm of darkness, sin, and death into the sphere of light, righteousness, and life; from the authority of Satan to the authority of God; out of the authority of darkness, the kingdom of Satan, into the kingdom of the Son of God's love, being restricted and ruled in His divine love under the authority in resurrection; and out of Adam into Christ. In Adam we were constituted sinners, we were condemned, and we were dead. In Christ, however, we have been constituted righteous and justified unto life; we have been transferred out of the bondage, demand, and curse of the law into the freedom, supply, and blessing of grace; and we have been delivered out of the evil and crooked generation, that is, the religious generation, into Christ and the church.

QUESTIONS

1. What are the results of the believers' being transferred?

2. Briefly state the meaning of the believers' being delivered out of the authority of darkness into the kingdom of the Son of God's love.

3. Briefly state the meaning of the believers' being delivered out of Adam into Christ.

4. Briefly explain the significance of the believers' being transferred from law to grace.

5. Briefly explain the significance of the believers' being delivered out of the evil age into Christ and the church.

MADE A NEW CREATION

(5)

BEING FREED

OUTLINE

I. Concerning sin:
  A. Freed from sins.
  B. Freed from the power of sin:
    1. Having the real freedom.
    2. No longer serving sin as slaves.
    3. Freed from sin.

II. Concerning law:
  A. Freed from law.
  B. Freed from the bondage of law:
    1. Freed from the yoke of slavery.
    2. No longer slaves but sons.
    3. Freed from the labor and burden under the law.

III. Concerning self:
  A. Freed from the flesh.
  B. Freed from the old man.

IV. Concerning Satan:
  A. Freed from Satan's oppression.
  B. Freed from the authority of darkness.

V. Concerning the world:
  A. Freed from the world's temptations, course, and current.

B. Freed from the religious world and the elements of the world:
  1. Freed from the religious world.
  2. Freed from the elements of the world.
C. Freed from the vain manner of life.

TEXT

In Lesson Thirty-six we saw the freedom which we receive when we are redeemed. In this lesson we will continue to see the freedom which we enjoy when we are made a new creation. To be freed is to be released. When we are regenerated, receive the Holy Spirit and God's eternal life, and are renewed and transferred, we are freed, released, from all bondage of sin, law, self, Satan, and the world.

No matter how well-educated a person is, how high his position, and how good his conduct, as long as he is a person of the world, he is a person under bondage. Not only is he serving under sin as a slave and as a captive (John 8:34; Rom. 6:17; 7:14), but he is also being held under law (Rom. 7:6). Furthermore, in his self he is entangled with the flesh (Rom. 7:24) and bound by the old man, and he is even under the hand of Satan (1 John 5:19; Acts 26:18), caught (2 Tim. 2:26), bound (Luke 13:16), and oppressed by him (Acts 10:38). Lastly, he is under the bondage of the world's temptations (1 John 2:15-16), course (Eph. 2:2), and current (Rom. 12:2). Hence, man needs deliverance that he may be freed, released, from all kinds of bondage.

Now we will see the various aspects of the freedom that the believers enjoy after they have received God's salvation.

I. CONCERNING SIN

The first kind of bondage to man is sin. Man under sin is just like a slave; he is dominated and manipulated by sin and has no freedom whatsoever.

A. Freed from Sins

Matthew 1:21 says, "He [Jesus] shall save His people from their sins." We were sinking in sins and could not rescue ourselves, even if we tried. However, through incarnation the Lord Jesus came into the world to be our

Savior (John 1:14). He was God incarnated as a man, that in His human body, through the redemption of His death and the power of His resurrection, He might deliver us from sins that we might become transcendent and free.

B. Freed from the Power of Sin

1. Having the Real Freedom

Once we are saved, we are delivered from the power of sin and we enjoy real freedom. Although people today greatly promote freedom and all like to enjoy freedom, they are under sin's domination and are without freedom. They indulge in the enjoyment of sin as if they are following after their heart's desires. But in fact, they are going contrary to their own wish and acting against their own conscience. Serving sin as slaves, as captives (John 8:34), they have no real freedom. It is not until they receive the Lord Jesus as their Savior that they are really free. This is because the Lord Jesus as the Son of God has the life of God in Him. When man receives Him as the Savior, the life of God which is in Him enters into man as the power of life that enables man to resist the enslaving sin and thus be freed from its power and enjoy the real freedom (John 8:36).

Furthermore, John 8:32 says that "the truth shall make you free" (ASV). The truth is Christ Himself as the reality of the divine things (John 14:6). Since Christ is the embodiment of God (Col. 2:9), He is the reality of what God is. When Christ comes into us as life, He shines within us as light (John 1:4; 8:12), which brings the divine element as reality into us. This reality, which is the divine element imparted into us and realized by us, sets us free from the slavery of sin by the divine life as the light of men.

2. No Longer Serving Sin as Slaves

When we are delivered from the power of sin, we no longer serve sin as slaves. Romans 6:6 says that "our old man has been crucified with Him...that we should no longer serve sin as slaves." Since our sinning old man has been crucified and has died with the Lord Jesus, we are spontaneously freed from sin and no longer serve sin as slaves (Rom. 6:6-7). We escape the penalty of sin through the Lord's vicarious death on the cross; we are freed from the domination of sin through our co-death with the Lord on the cross. Hence, the Lord's cross has delivered us and set us free from these two aspects of sin.

3. Freed from Sin

When we are delivered and set free from the power of sin, we are also set free from sin. Romans 6:14 says, "For sin shall not lord it over you, for you are not under law but under grace." Sin lords it over man through the law, for without law sin is dead, but when the law comes, sin revives (Rom. 7:8-9). Before we were saved, the more we tried to keep the law by ourselves, the more we sensed that sin was lording it over us, making it impossible for us to be freed from its power. After we are saved, the Lord's salvation causes us to have the divine life, to be joined to the Lord, and to be crucified with Him. Therefore, we no longer keep the law of God by ourselves, but we enjoy the grace of God by the divine life. Thus, we no longer live under law but under grace, and sin can no longer lord it over us. Hence, we are delivered from the power of sin—we are freed from sin (Rom. 6:14, 18, 22).

II. CONCERNING LAW

A. Freed from Law

One reason that God gave the law was to guard His chosen people until Christ came (Gal. 3:23). When the fullness of the time came, God sent forth His Son, come of a woman, come under law, that He might redeem those under law, that they might receive the sonship and become the sons of God (Gal. 4:4-5). Therefore, Christ's redemption has redeemed us not only out of the curse of the law (Gal. 3:13) but also out of the custody of the law, bringing us into the divine sonship to enjoy the divine life and obtain the real freedom.

We were also under the domination and bondage of the law (Rom. 7:1-2). However, Christ has brought us with Him into His death on the cross that we might die to the law. Hence, we are discharged from the law and are not required to answer to the law any longer. This is because the law lords it over a man only while he lives, but when he dies he is freed from the domination of the law. Furthermore, Christ has also brought us with Him into His resurrection that we may receive His life and enjoy God's grace forever. Hence, we are not under law but under grace (Rom. 6:14); that is, we are not being controlled under law, but we are enjoying freedom under grace.

B. Freed from the Bondage of Law

1. Freed from the Yoke of Slavery

Christ has set us free from the bondage of law, that is, from the yoke of slavery. Galatians 5:1 says, "For freedom Christ has set us free;... do not be again entangled with a yoke of slavery." Freedom here denotes freedom from the slavery of law. We were under law, entangled with a yoke of slavery, the bondage of law. Through His redeeming death and life-imparting resurrection, Christ has set us free, delivering us from the enslaving yoke of the law that we may enjoy freedom.

2. No Longer Slaves but Sons

Since we have been set free from the enslaving yoke of the law, we are no longer slaves but sons (Gal. 4:7). As slaves under law, we were without freedom. But when we receive Jesus, the Son of God, as our Savior, the Spirit of God's Son comes into us to impart the divine life to us and make us the sons of God. Hence, we are no longer under law as slaves to ordinances, bound by letters; we are under grace as sons in life, enjoying freedom in life. This freedom includes liberation from obligation, that is, liberation from the obligation of the law and its ordinances, practices, and regulations; satisfaction because of an adequate supply and support; true rest; and the enjoyment of Christ, the enjoyment of all that He is. Since we have such a freedom, we are no longer under any kind of enslavement, much less under the domination of law.

3. Freed from the Labor and Burden under the Law

God's salvation sets us free not only from the law and its bondage but also from the labor and burden of the law. In Matthew 11:28 the Lord Jesus says, "Come to Me all who labor and are burdened, and I will give you rest." This promise was spoken especially to those who were trying to keep the law. The labor here refers in particular to the labor of striving to keep the commandments of the law and religious regulations, and it also refers to the labor of carrying out any work and responsibility. Whoever labors thus is always heavily burdened. The Lord is calling this kind of people to come to Him for rest, that is, to enjoy rest by being set free from labor and burden under the law and religion or under any work and responsibility.

III. CONCERNING SELF

A. Freed from the Flesh

The flesh is the corrupted human body. When God created man, man had only the physical body, not the flesh. At that time, neither sin nor lust was in the human body; it was simply a created body. However, when Satan tempted man to eat of the fruit of the tree of knowledge of good and evil, Satan and his sinful life, which were signified by the fruit, entered into the human body, causing the human body to be transmuted and corrupted and thus to become the flesh. In the Bible this flesh is called "the body of sin" (Rom. 6:6) and "the body of this death" (Rom. 7:24). Although such a fallen flesh is utterly powerless in doing good, it is exceedingly active in committing sin. Hence, the flesh is a great bondage and entanglement to man, and it is something which man cannot rid himself of. After we have believed in Christ, we are transferred into Christ. In Him we are circumcised with a circumcision not made with hands, in the putting off of the body of the flesh, in the circumcision of Christ (Col. 2:11). The circumcision of Christ refers to the proper baptism, which puts off the body of the flesh by the effectual virtue of the death of Christ, thus terminating our flesh. Hence, we are no longer in the entanglement of the flesh; rather, we have been freed from the flesh.

B. Freed from the Old Man

The fallen man has not only the problem of the flesh but also the problem of the old man. In fact, the two—the flesh and the old man—are one. In the old creation we are the old man. When the old man is lived out and expressed, it is the flesh. Therefore, both the old man and the flesh refer to our very being. As to the objective fact, we are the old man; as to the subjective experience, we are the flesh. The flesh is the living out and the expression of the old man; that is, the flesh is our experience of the old man. When we are baptized, we put off not only the flesh but also the old man (Col. 3:9). Our old man was crucified with Christ (Rom. 6:6) and was buried in baptism (Rom. 6:4a). We experience this putting off by the life of Christ, who has passed through death and resurrection. Hence, we are no longer entangled with the flesh nor encumbered with the old man.

IV. CONCERNING SATAN

A. Freed from Satan's Oppression

People in the world today have been captured by the Devil and have fallen into his snare (2 Tim. 2:26). They have lost their freedom and they have no way to rescue themselves. Satan utilizes many things, such as sin, money, and pleasure, to deceive and capture man. Moreover, he uses sickness and affliction to bind man (Luke

13:16) and to oppress man (Acts 10:38), thus depriving man of his freedom. However, the Lord Jesus came to set the captives free and to release those who are oppressed. Christ destroyed Satan through His death in the flesh on the cross (Heb. 2:14), thus setting us free, releasing us, from Satan's hand.

B. Freed from the Authority of Darkness

Christ has set us free not only from Satan's oppression but also from his authority of darkness (Col. 1:13; Acts 26:18). Satan's authority of darkness is his kingdom. People are controlled and held by Satan in his kingdom. When we were sinners, we were held in Satan's kingdom of darkness, controlled and cruelly treated under his authority. However, since we have received God's salvation, we have been delivered out of Satan's kingdom of darkness, Satan's authority, by Christ through His death in the flesh and His resurrection life, and we also have been transferred into the kingdom of His own light (Col. 1:13; Acts 26:18), that we may enjoy freedom in the light.

V. CONCERNING THE WORLD

A. Freed from the World's Temptations, Course, and Current

Because man is born into the world, which is degraded and which renounces and even resists God, man is trapped in its snare and dominion. Man simply cannot free himself from the usurpation and enslavement of the world's temptations, such as the lust of the flesh, the lust of the eyes, and the vainglory of the present life (1 John 2:15-16). Neither can he free himself from the world's course (Eph. 2:2) and from the world's fashion, the world's current (Rom. 12:2). When we are joined to the Lord organically by our believing and being baptized, through our co-death and co-resurrection with Him we are set free from the world's power, or we may say from its charm, and are brought into a new realm to live the life of the new man in God's new creation.

B. Freed from the Religious World and the Elements of the World

1. Freed from the Religious World

Galatians 1:4 says that Christ "gave Himself for our sins, that He might rescue us out of the present evil age, according to the will of our God and Father." An age is a part of the world as the satanic system. The present evil age, according to the context of Galatians, refers to the religious world, the Jewish religion, because in 6:14-15 Paul pointed out that the circumcision practiced by the Jewish religion was a part of the world. Therefore, the purpose of Christ's giving Himself for our sins was to rescue us out of the evil age, the religious world which is a part of the satanic system, and to thus set us free.

2. Freed from the Elements of the World

Colossians 2:20 says, "If you died with Christ from the elements of the world . . . ." The elements of the world refer to the religions, ordinances, and philosophies (Col. 2:8, 21-23) of the world. Actually, all the religions, ordinances, and philosophies of the world are inventions of man's wisdom and cleverness through Satan's initiation that man may be bound. Since we have been joined to Christ by believing into Him, through our co-death with Him we have been rescued from the world. Hence, we have also been rescued from the bondage of the worldly religions, ordinances, and philosophies that we may enjoy the freedom of the salvation in His life.

C. Freed from the Vain Manner of Life

First Peter 1:18-19 says that "you were redeemed . . . from your vain manner of life handed down from your fathers . . . with precious blood . . . of Christ." The vain manner of life of people today was handed down from their fathers, generation after generation, and it is difficult for them to be freed from it. However, Christ accomplished redemption on the cross, shedding His precious blood to redeem us back to God. Hence, we have been delivered from the vain manner of life handed down through the generations, that we may be free to live out a sanctified life that expresses God in His holiness.

SUMMARY

To be freed is to be released. The freedom which the believers enjoy when they are made a new creation is their being freed, released, from all bondage of sin, law, self, Satan, and the world. When Christ sets us free, He first saves us from sins and from the power of sin that we may have the real freedom, that we may no longer serve sin as slaves, and that we may be freed from sin. He also saves us from law and its bondage that we may be no longer under law as slaves of ordinances, bound by letters, but under grace as sons in life, enjoying freedom in life, and that we may be freed from labor under law and religion or any work and responsibility to enjoy rest. Furthermore, He saves us from the flesh and the old man so that we are no longer entangled with the flesh or encumbered with the old man. He also saves us out of Satan's oppression and his authority of darkness. Moreover, through His death in the flesh on the cross, He has destroyed Satan, thus setting us free from Satan's hand, delivering us out of his kingdom of darkness, and transferring us into Christ's kingdom of light that we may enjoy freedom in the light. Lastly, He has rescued us from the world's temptations, course, and current, from the religious world and the elements of the world, and from the vain manner of life handed down from our fathers, that we may be free to live out a sanctified life that expresses God in His holiness.

QUESTIONS

1. Briefly discuss how the believers are saved from sins and from the power of sin.

2. Briefly explain how the believers are delivered from law and its bondage.

3. How did the human body become the flesh by being transmuted and corrupted? What is the relationship between the flesh and the old man? How are the believers freed from the entanglement of the flesh and the encumbrance of the old man?

4. Briefly explain how the believers are freed from Satan's oppression and his authority of darkness.

5. Briefly explain how the believers are released from the various aspects of the world.

SALVATION

OUTLINE

I. The source of salvation:
   A. God's love.
   B. God's mercy.
   C. God's grace.

II. The accomplishment of salvation:
   A. Of God the Father.
   B. In God the Son.
   C. Through God the Spirit.

III. The means of salvation:
   A. God's calling.
   B. The Spirit's sanctification.
   C. Christ's redemption.
   D. Union with the Triune God.
   E. The Spirit's regeneration.

IV. The way to be saved:
   A. Believing.
   B. Calling.
   C. Confessing.
   D. Being baptized.

V. The effect of salvation.

TEXT

In the initial stage of God's full salvation the believers experience God's calling, the Spirit's sanctification, their repentance, believing, and being baptized, Christ's redemption, their union with the Triune God, and the Spirit's regeneration. Hence, they are saved, that is, they have received God's eternal salvation. Concerning salvation, the Bible speaks of at least five kinds: eternal salvation, daily salvation, environmental salvation, salvation of the body, and salvation of the soul. In this lesson we will cover only the first kind of salvation, that is, eternal salvation.

I. THE SOURCE OF SALVATION

A. God's Love

We have been saved because of God's love. God's love is the source of God's salvation. If God had not loved us, we would not have received salvation. God's heart is love, and His heart so loved us "that He gave us His only begotten Son" (John 3:16) to prepare salvation for us. His great love caused Him to love us, who were not only sinners but also dead ones, those who were deeply fallen and were dead in offenses and sins. Thus, He made us alive and caused us to ascend to the heavens together with Christ (Eph. 2:4-6). Therefore, our salvation is because of God's love.

B. God's Mercy

We have been saved according to God's mercy (Titus 3:5). According to our true condition, we not only were short of righteous deeds, but we also were full of sins and were therefore unworthy of God's love. But God not only loves us; He is also rich in mercy (Eph. 2:4). His mercy reaches farther than His love. Because of His mercy, His love was able to reach us and to visit us, the fallen and unbecoming ones, lifting us up from an undeserving position that we might be worthy to enjoy His love. His love prepared salvation for us, while His mercy caused

Him to bestow His salvation upon us, the undeserving ones.

C. God's Grace

We have been saved by God's grace (Eph. 2:8-9). Because God loves us, He has given us grace. This grace has become the source of our eternal salvation. We have been saved by grace, which comes out of God's love and which is through His mercy. This grace is not of ourselves; it is the gift of God. It is also not of our works, which have nothing to do with our eternal salvation (2 Tim. 1:9). We were saved apart from our works; in fact, we were saved altogether according to God's grace, which came to us through the Lord Jesus (John 1:17). By this grace He accomplished salvation for us, performing everything that was necessary for us to be saved. Therefore, we have been saved by God's grace and not by our works.

II. THE ACCOMPLISHMENT OF SALVATION

The source of our salvation is God's love, God's mercy, and God's grace, while the accomplishment of our salvation is by the Triune God. It is the Triune God who saved us and became our Savior: God the Father planned, God the Son accomplished what the Father planned, and God the Spirit applies to us what God the Son accomplished (Eph. 1:3-14). Therefore, the Bible addresses God particularly as "God our Savior" (1 Tim. 1:1; 4:10) and "our Savior God" (1 Tim. 2:3; Titus 1:3; 2:10; 3:4).

The three parables spoken by the Lord Jesus in Luke 15 unveil and depict the work of the divine Trinity in bringing fallen sinners back, through the Son by the Spirit, to the Father. The Son came in His humanity as the Shepherd to find the sinner as a lost sheep and bring him back home. The Spirit seeks the sinner as a woman seeks carefully one lost coin until she finds it. And the Father receives the repenting and returned sinner as a certain man receives his prodigal son. The entire divine Trinity treasures the sinner and participates in bringing him back to God. Therefore, the Triune God Himself is the Accomplisher of our salvation; He is the One who completed the work of salvation.

A. Of God the Father

The work of salvation which God accomplished in His divine Trinity is firstly of God the Father (2 Thes. 2:13). God the Father chose us from the beginning; that is, before the foundation of the world and in His sovereign ordination, He foreknew, chose, and predestinated us to receive His salvation. Since He is the origin and source of salvation, it is of God the Father that we are saved.

B. In God the Son

The work of salvation which God accomplished in His divine Trinity is in God the Son. As the embodiment of the Triune God, the Son was sent by the Father (1 John 4:14) into the world as a man to save sinners (1 Tim. 1:15). He passed through incarnation, human living, death, resurrection, and ascension, thus accomplishing an eternal redemption. On the one hand, He terminated the negative things, such as sin, the flesh, the old man, Satan and the world belonging to him, the old creation, and all separating ordinances of the law; on the other hand, He released the divine life. Thus, He is able to redeem us who have believed into Him. Furthermore, in resurrection He brought us into a life relationship, an organic union, with God, that we might participate in all that God is and has. Hence, we are saved in God the Son.

C. Through God the Spirit

The work of salvation which God accomplished in His divine Trinity is through God the Spirit (Titus 3:5). God the Spirit is the ultimate consummation of the processed Triune God, the reaching of the Triune God to us to apply that which the Father planned and that which the Son accomplished. First, by enlightening and seeking man He sanctifies the fallen man unto the obedience of faith in Christ's redemption. This is illustrated by the second parable in Luke 15, which speaks of a woman who lights a lamp, sweeps the house, and seeks carefully until she finds the lost coin. This is also what the Lord Jesus was referring to in John 16:8, where He said that when the Spirit comes, He will convict the world concerning sin, concerning righteousness, and concerning judgment, that men may repent and turn to God, believe into the Lord Jesus, and be regenerated. Furthermore, the Spirit washes and renews us in the divine element to make us a new creation with the divine nature that, having been justified by the grace of the Lord Jesus Christ, we may become heirs of God in His eternal life (Titus 3:7), inheriting all that the Triune God is to us. Therefore, our salvation is of God the Father, in God the Son, and through God the Spirit. It is the Triune God Himself who accomplished this work of salvation.

III. THE MEANS OF SALVATION

The source of our salvation is God's love, God's mercy, and God's grace; the accomplishment of our salvation is by the Triune God; and the means of our salvation is through God's calling, the Spirit's sanctification, Christ's redemption, our union with the Triune God, and the Spirit's regeneration.

A. God's Calling

We are saved, first, through God's calling. God's calling is the first thing that God accomplishes in His chosen ones in the initial stage of His full salvation. This is God's new beginning, in which He calls men out of the created Adamic race and transfers them into the called Abrahamic race, and out of the life of the old creation into the life of the new creation, that the believers may come out of darkness and enter into the marvelous light of God, out of the death-realm of Satan's darkness into the life-realm of God's marvelous light, and become a people made holy unto God. It is through God's calling that we receive God's salvation. Therefore, we are saved through God's calling.

B. The Spirit's Sanctification

We are saved through the Spirit's sanctification. After God calls man, the Holy Spirit comes to separate man, to sanctify man, that man may repent and turn to God unto the obedience of faith in Christ's redemption. The Holy Spirit sanctifies the fallen men by enlightening and seeking them, convicting them concerning sin, concerning righteousness, and concerning judgment, thus causing them to repent and turn to God and to receive God's salvation. Therefore, we are saved through the Spirit's sanctification.

C. Christ's Redemption

We are saved through Christ's redemption. Christ died on the cross to accomplish an eternal redemption for man. When we believe into Christ, we are redeemed; that is, we are forgiven of our sins, freed, washed, sanctified, justified, and reconciled to God. As a result, we who once belonged to God but became lost, and who became God's enemies because of our fall, are recovered and accepted by God. Hence, we are saved through Christ's redemption.

D. Union with the Triune God

We are saved also through our union with the Triune God. After we repent, believe, and are baptized, we are joined to the processed Triune God. Through our union with God the Father we have His divine life and nature, being related to Him in life and joined to Him in nature, thus producing an organic union. Through our union with God the Son we have been put in Him and He in us; thus we have become one with Him, sharing with Him the same life, nature, living, and activities. And through our union with God the Spirit we have received Him into us essentially for our existence, being, life, and living; we also have received Him as the Spirit of power upon us economically for our spiritual work and function. Through such a wonderful union with the Triune God we enjoy all the blessings of His salvation. Hence, we are saved through our union with the Triune God.

E. The Spirit's Regeneration

Our salvation is through the Spirit's regeneration (John 3:5). Christ's redemption solves the outward problems between us and God. However, besides having problems with God outwardly, we also have problems inwardly in life and nature. Hence, when we believe and are baptized, God not only solves our outward problems through Christ's redemption but also imparts His life and nature into us through the Spirit's regeneration. Therefore, we are saved through the Spirit's regeneration.

IV. THE WAY TO BE SAVED

The way for the believers to be saved is to believe, to call, to confess, and to be baptized. These four matters joined together form one complete step for the believers to receive the Lord's salvation. When we have these four items, we are fully saved.

A. Believing

We are saved by God's grace and also through our faith, that is, our believing (Eph. 2:8). Although there is God's grace, without our believing, we still cannot be saved. By His grace, God has prepared and accomplished salvation for us; by our believing, we receive that which has been prepared and accomplished. By His grace, God gives us salvation; by our believing, we receive that which has been given. If there is only the preparation by God's grace but not the appropriation by our believing, or if there is only the giving by God's grace but not the receiving by our

believing, we still cannot obtain God's salvation. In order
to obtain God's salvation, we must apply and receive it by
believing. This is the way, the step, for us to obtain God's
salvation.

B. Calling

Once a person believes in the Lord, he will spontaneously
call on the Lord (Rom. 10:14). Although he cannot see the
Lord, a person can call upon His name. The Lord's name is
the Lord Himself. Hence, to call on the Lord's name is to
call on the Lord Himself. Therefore, whoever calls upon the
name of the Lord shall be saved by Him.

C. Confessing

When a person believes into the Lord, he must confess
the Lord (Rom. 10:10). When we believe into the Lord, we
believe in our heart in the Lord as our Savior; when we
confess, we confess with our mouth the Lord as Lord. To
believe into the Lord is primarily before God, whereas to
confess with the mouth is mainly before men. Once we
believe into the Lord in our heart, we are saved. But we
must confess with our mouth before men in order to show
forth the fact that we have believed into the Lord and are
saved. Merely to believe into the Lord in our heart without
confessing with our mouth indicates that there is a
problem not only before men but also before God. Hence, in
order that we may be thoroughly saved, we must believe in
our heart and confess with our mouth.

D. Being Baptized

He who believes and is baptized shall be saved (Mark
16:16). Faith is related to man's salvation, because man is
saved by believing; likewise, baptism is also related to
man's salvation, because man is saved also by being
baptized. To believe is to exercise the inward faith to
receive the Lord's salvation, whereas to be baptized is to
take an outward action to partake of the Lord's salvation.

To believe and be baptized constitutes one complete step by which man receives the Lord's salvation. To believe without being baptized is to receive the Lord's salvation by taking only a half step. The Lord's salvation consists of many elements, some of which man must apply and receive by believing, while others man must enter into and partake of by being baptized. If a person believes but is not baptized, he can receive only a partial salvation; he cannot receive the Lord's complete salvation. To receive the Lord's complete salvation, a person must believe and be baptized.

V. THE EFFECT OF SALVATION

Once a person is saved by believing in the Lord, he is forgiven of his sins and is delivered from God's judgment and condemnation (John 3:18; 5:24), from the curse of the law (Gal. 3:13), from God's wrath (Rom. 5:9; John 3:36; 1 Thes. 1:10), and from the fear and slavery of death (Heb. 2:14-15), thus escaping eternal perdition (John 3:16). Moreover, having been born of God and having received God's eternal life and His Holy Spirit, he is delivered from sins (Matt. 1:21) and the power of sin (John 8:34, 36; Rom. 6:6), and from law (Gal. 4:4-5; Rom. 7:6) and the bondage of law (Gal. 5:1; 4:7). He is also freed from the flesh (Col. 2:11), the old man (Col. 3:9), the oppression of Satan (Luke 4:18; Acts 10:38), the power and charm of the world, the religious world and its ordinances (Gal. 1:4; 6:14-15; Col. 2:20), and the vain manner of life handed down from his fathers (1 Pet. 1:18). Thus, he is fully set free (John 8:36) and is no longer under any bondage or confinement.

SUMMARY

The source of our salvation is God's love, God's mercy, and God's grace. The accomplishment of our salvation is by the Triune God: God the Father foreknew, chose, and predestinated us to receive His salvation; God the Son accomplished redemption and released the divine life; and God the Spirit convicted us concerning sin, righteousness, and judgment that we might repent and turn to God, believe into the Lord Jesus, and be regenerated, and He also is making us a new creation with the divine life by washing and renewing us with the divine elements. We are saved through God's calling, the Spirit's sanctification, Christ's redemption, our union with the Triune God, and the Spirit's regeneration. In order to be fully saved, we must pass through the complete step of believing, calling, confessing, and being baptized. Once we are saved by believing in the Lord, we are delivered from God's judgment, condemnation, and wrath, from the curse of the law, and from the fear and slavery of death, thus escaping eternal perdition. Moreover, we are released from sins, the power of sin, the law, the bondage of the law, the flesh, the old man, the oppression of Satan, the power and charm of the world, the religious world and its ordinances, and the vain manner of life handed down from our fathers. Thus we are fully set free and are no longer under any bondage or confinement.

QUESTIONS

1. Briefly state the source of salvation.

2. Briefly explain how the Triune God accomplishes the work of salvation.

3. What are the means by which the believers are saved?

4. What is the way for the believers to be saved?

5. Briefly state the effect of salvation.

THE ASSURANCE AND SECURITY OF SALVATION

OUTLINE

I. Receiving salvation at the moment of believing:
   A. Being redeemed.
   B. Being regenerated.
   C. Passing out of death into life.

II. The assurance of salvation:
   A. By the Word of God.
   B. By the Spirit's witnessing with our spirit.
   C. By our loving the brothers.

III. The security of salvation:
   A. By the invariable God.
   B. By God's unchanging will.
   C. By God's inseparable love.
   D. By God's irrevocable calling.
   E. By God's unchallengeable justification.
   F. By God's almighty hand.
   G. By God's eternal life.
   H. By God's new covenant.
   I. By Christ's perfect, complete, and eternal redemption.
   J. By Christ's eternal salvation.
   K. By Christ's almighty hand.
   L. By Christ's unfailing promise.

TEXT

In this lesson we will see the assurance and security of salvation. Among today's Christians there are many different views concerning salvation. Some people consider that it is impossible to know today that we are saved, while others think that after we are saved we may still perish. The Bible shows us, however, that our salvation is not a matter of speculation, nor is it a matter of uncertainty. Rather, it is something which can be confirmed with assurance and which we may know with full confidence. Moreover, our salvation is secure. Once we have it, we have it eternally. It can never be shaken or changed.

I. RECEIVING SALVATION
AT THE MOMENT OF BELIEVING

Many people consider that believing is a present matter and that receiving salvation is a future matter, that is, that a man believes today and will be saved in the future. However, the Bible tells us clearly and definitely that at the moment a man believes, he is saved (Acts 16:31; Rom. 10:10). It is not that he will be saved in the future, but that he is already saved today. He is saved at the very time that he believes. Salvation immediately follows believing, for there is no space of time between the two.

A. Being Redeemed

When a person believes, he is saved. The Bible clearly reveals that when a person believes, he is forgiven of his sins (Acts 10:43; 1 John 2:12), freed (John 3:18; Gal. 3:13), washed (1 Cor. 6:11; Acts 15:9), sanctified (1 Cor. 6:11; Acts 26:18), justified (Rom. 5:1; 3:28, 30; Gal. 3:8, 24; Acts 13:39), and reconciled to God (Rom. 5:10). Therefore, when we believe, we are redeemed and we are saved.

B. Being Regenerated

When a person believes, he is not only redeemed but also regenerated. John 1:12-13 clearly points out that

anyone who believes in the Lord is born of God and
becomes a child of God. Hence, as long as a man believes
into the Lord Jesus, he is regenerated, he has God's eternal
life, and he will not perish forever (John 3:15-16); that is, he
is saved.

C. Passing Out of Death into Life

When a person believes, he passes out of death into life.
John 3:16 and 5:24 tell us that he who believes has eternal
life, and he will not be judged nor will he perish; he has
passed out of death into life. Hence, as long as we believe,
we have eternal life, and we are no longer condemned or
judged; we have passed out of death into life.

The above three points clearly prove that we need only
to believe, and we are saved immediately.

II. THE ASSURANCE OF SALVATION

A. By the Word of God

First, the assurance of our salvation is based on the
Word of God (1 John 5:13). Through the Bible God tells us
and testifies to us concerning the redemption which He has
accomplished for us through His Son; through the Bible He
also reveals to us and bears witness concerning the
salvation that has been wrought in us through the Spirit in
His Son. Therefore, by the word of God in the Scriptures we
know that we are saved. The Scripture verses quoted in the
foregoing section concerning our receiving salvation at the
moment we believe are not only God's revelation and
promise to us, but they are also His covenant and written
evidence to us. By His word in the covenant and by the
written evidence we can know, even with confidence and
assurance, that once we believe in the Lord, we are
forgiven of our sins, freed, washed, sanctified, justified,
and reconciled to God, we have eternal life and shall not
perish, we have passed out of death into life, and we are
saved.

Man acquires an inheritance by a testament. The

written words of the covenant in the Bible were left to us by the Lord as a testament (Heb. 9:15-16), by which we may inherit the blessings of His salvation. When a person intends to bequeath his possessions, he lists his possessions in a will and bequeaths them to the inheritor. Likewise, the Lord has given His salvation to us by including it in His testament—the Bible. A man receives a bequest according to the clear stipulations expressed in the will, not according to his own consideration or imagination. Likewise, we inherit the Lord's salvation according to the plain statements contained in the Bible, His testament, not according to our own imagination or sensation. Hence, since we have the Bible as an outward proof to us, we do not need our feelings; according to the plain statements, we can assuredly know that we have received grace, that we are saved. This is a proof that is outside of us, which we may call the outward proof.

B. By the Spirit's Witnessing with Our Spirit

The assurance of our salvation is based on the Spirit's witnessing with our spirit (Rom. 8:16). We not only have the Word of God outside of us confirming the fact that we have been saved, but we also have the Spirit within us witnessing with our spirit that we are the children of God and that God is our Father. Everyone who believes in the Lord enjoys addressing God as "Abba, Father." It is a spontaneous matter for us to call God "Abba, Father." Moreover, every time we call Him "Abba, Father," we feel sweet and comfortable within. This is because we are children begotten of God, we have God's life, and the Spirit of God's Son has entered into us. Concerning our father in the flesh, it is spontaneous and sweet for us to call him "Father." Therefore, since we enjoy calling God "Abba, Father," and do it spontaneously, even with a sweet and comfortable sensation, this proves that we have God's life and are children begotten of God. Hence, by the Spirit's inner witnessing with our spirit we can know with certainty that we are God's children and that we are saved. This is a proof within us, which we may call the inward proof.

C. By Our Loving the Brothers

The assurance of salvation is based on the fact that we love the brothers. First John 3:14 says, "We know that we have passed out of death into life, because we love the brothers." Since God is love (1 John 4:16) and since we have His life, we surely have the divine love. Furthermore, since we have been begotten of God, we certainly love those who have been begotten of Him (1 John 5:1). When a saved one sees a brother in the Lord, he has an affection for him and even loves him in such a manner that is incomprehensible to himself. Therefore, our love toward the brothers in the Lord is a proof by which we know that we have been saved. This is a proof of our experience of life, which we may call the proof of love. By our believing— believing in the Lord—we have life and have passed out of death into life; by our loving—loving the brothers—we know that we have life and that we have passed out of death into life.

Therefore, by the clear words of the Bible, by the sensation in our spirit, and by the experience of love, we can know with certainty that we are saved.

III. THE SECURITY OF SALVATION

Now we will go on to see the security of salvation. Our salvation not only can be proved with assurance, but it is also secure. According to the revelation of the Bible, the security of salvation is demonstrated by the following twelve items:

A. By the Invariable God

First, our salvation is secured by the invariable God. James 1:17 says that with the Father there is "no variableness or shadow cast by turning." James clearly indicates that God is not variable, and with Him there is no shadow cast by turning. He is not like the heavenly bodies, which turn and whose shadows also change, as seen in the waxing and waning of the moon while it revolves around the earth and in the eclipsing of the sun by the moon. God is secure; He is not variable, not changeable. Therefore, since He has saved us, our salvation can never be changed, and we shall never perish.

B. By God's Unchanging Will

Our salvation is secured by God's unchanging will. Hebrews 6:17 speaks of "the unchangeableness of His [God's] counsel." Since God's counsel, that is, God's will, is unchangeable, the fact that He chose us and predestinated us before the foundation of the world that we might receive His salvation (Eph. 1:4-5, 11) is also unchangeable. Since He chose and predestinated us in eternity past that we might receive sonship and become His inheritance, He will carry it out and will not fail. Hence, our salvation is secure.

C. By God's Inseparable Love

Our salvation is also secured by God's inseparable love. First John 4:10 says, "In this is love, not that we have loved God, but that He loved us, and sent His Son a propitiation concerning our sins." If we are saved because we love God, then our salvation is not reliable. However, we are saved because God loved us; that is, our salvation is of God's love. Since God is unchanging, His love is also unalterable. Moreover, His love toward us is an inseparable love (Rom. 8:39). Hence, nothing can separate us from His love. Neither death nor life, neither angels nor demons, neither things present nor things to come, shall be able to separate us from the love of God. Because of God's inseparable love, His salvation within us will never fail; it is forever secure and unchanging.

D. By God's Irrevocable Calling

Our salvation is secured by God's irrevocable calling. Romans 11:29 says that the calling of God is irrevocable. Since God's calling comes out of His invariable being and is according to His unchanging will, it is irrevocable and unalterable. Hence, the salvation which God has called us to receive is also unalterable. Therefore, according to God's calling, our salvation is eternally secure.

E. By God's Unchallengeable Justification

It is because of His love that God gave His only begotten Son, the Lord Jesus, to us to be our Savior (John 3:16), and it is by the grace of God that the Lord Jesus accomplished redemption for us (Heb. 2:9). However, after the Lord Jesus was judged on the cross by God's righteousness on our behalf and thereby satisfied God's righteous requirement, we who believe in Him are justified according to God's righteousness to show forth God's righteousness (Rom. 3:26). If the Lord Jesus had not satisfied God's righteous requirement on our behalf, even though, because of His love, God desires to grant us the grace of forgiveness, He could not forgive us or justify us, because that would make Him unrighteous. However, since the Lord Jesus has satisfied God's righteous requirement on our behalf, God can—and He must—forgive us and justify us according to His righteousness; otherwise, He would make Himself unrighteous. Hence, bound by His righteousness, God must justify us. Romans 8:33 says, "Who shall lay anything to the charge of God's elect? Shall God that justifieth?" (ASV, margin). Since God is bound by His righteousness, He must justify us; He cannot accuse us or condemn us any longer. God's righteousness is the foundation of God's throne (Psa. 89:14a, ASV). God's throne is securely established and cannot be shaken. Likewise, God's justification according to His righteousness is securely established and forever unchallengeable. Hence, our salvation is eternally secure.

F. By God's Almighty Hand

The security of our salvation rests on God's almighty hand. In John 10:29 the Lord said, "My Father who has given them to Me is greater than all, and no one can snatch them out of My Father's hand." Because God is greater than all, He is more powerful than anything. No one can snatch us out of His almighty hand. Hence, as far as God's almighty hand is concerned, our salvation is secure.

G. By God's Eternal Life

The security of our salvation also rests on God's eternal life. In John 10:28 the Lord said, "And I give to them eternal life, and they shall by no means perish forever." Eternal life is God's life. The Lord has given this life to us and has brought us into an eternal relationship with God, a relationship in life, so that we can never be separated from Him. Today, God's eternal life in us maintains the eternal security of our salvation so that we shall never perish.

H. By God's New Covenant

Our salvation is secured by the new covenant which God made with us (Heb. 8:8-12). This covenant was consummated through the redemption accomplished by the shedding of the blood of the Lord Jesus (Matt. 26:28; Luke 22:20). According to this covenant, God will forgive the sins of all those who believe in the Lord Jesus and will not remember their iniquities any longer; He will impart His laws into their mind and inscribe them on their hearts; He will be God to them and they will be a people to Him; and they all will know God and will not need others to teach them. At the same time, this covenant is an eternal covenant (Heb. 13:20), which will remain eternally and is effective eternally. Furthermore, because God is faithful and is One who keeps His covenant (Deut. 7:9), He will never break His covenant

(Psa. 89:34) but will fulfill it in us accordingly. Hence, His covenant, which cannot be annulled, guarantees the eternal security of our salvation.

I. By Christ's Perfect, Complete, and Eternal Redemption

Our salvation is also secured by Christ's eternal redemption, which is perfect and complete. Hebrews 10:14 says, "For by one offering He has perfected forever those who are sanctified." By offering Himself on the cross without blemish as the one sacrifice to God, Christ has accomplished an eternal redemption (Heb. 9:12; 10:10, 12). Hence, this redemption is eternally perfect and complete, without any blemish or shortcoming. Through Christ's eternal redemption we, the sanctified ones, have been perfected eternally. No one can condemn us any longer (Rom. 8:34), nor can anyone nullify the perfect, complete, and eternal redemption which Christ has accomplished for us. Hence, our salvation is eternally secure.

J. By Christ's Eternal Salvation

We are saved with security by Christ's eternal salvation. Hebrews 5:9 says that Christ "became to all them that obey Him the cause of eternal salvation." The salvation brought to us by Christ is an eternal salvation, all the effects, benefits, and issues of which are of an eternal nature, transcending the limitations of time. Our salvation, therefore, is eternally secure.

K. By Christ's Almighty Hand

The security of our salvation rests also on Christ's almighty hand. In John 10:28 the Lord said, "And I give to them eternal life, and they shall by no means perish forever, and no one shall snatch them out of My hand." Just as God's almighty hand is powerful, so also Christ's almighty hand is strong. Both are safeguards to our salvation. Eternal life shall never run out, and the hands of the Son and the Father shall never fail. Therefore, our salvation is eternally secure, and we shall never perish.

L. By Christ's Unfailing Promise

We are saved with security by Christ's unfailing promise. John 6:37 says, "All that the Father gives Me shall come to Me, and him that comes to Me I will by no means cast out." The Lord has promised that He will never cast out those who come to Him. Such a promise guarantees the eternal security of our salvation. Therefore, God has shown us in His Word from different angles that once we are saved, we are eternally saved, we are eternally perfected, we shall by no means perish eternally, and we are eternally secure.

SUMMARY

At the time that a man believes, he is redeemed and regenerated, and he passes out of death into life. Hence, at the moment a man believes, he is saved. Our salvation is assured, first, by the Word of God, that is, the plain statements of the Scriptures, the covenant which God has made with us and the testament which He has given to us. This is a proof that is outside of us, which we may call the outward proof. Second, our salvation is assured by the Spirit's witnessing with our spirit. This witnessing proves that we are the children of God and that God is our Father.

This is a proof within us, which we may call the inward proof. Third, our salvation is assured by our loving the brothers. Our love toward the brothers in the Lord is also a proof by which we know that we have been saved. This is a proof of our experience of life, which we may call the proof of love. Moreover, our salvation is secured by the invariable God, by God's unchanging will, by God's inseparable love, by God's irrevocable calling, by God's unchallengeable justification, by God's almighty hand, by God's eternal life, by God's new covenant, by Christ's perfect, complete, and eternal redemption, by Christ's eternal salvation, by Christ's almighty hand, and by Christ's unfailing promise. Therefore, God has shown us in His Word from different angles that once we are saved, we are eternally saved, we are eternally perfected, we shall by no means perish eternally, and we are eternally secure.

QUESTIONS

1. Quote the appropriate Scriptures to prove that a man is saved at the moment he believes.

2. What are the bases for the assurance of the believers' salvation?

3. What are the twelve items which make the believers' salvation secure?

THE CLEARANCE OF THE PAST

OUTLINE

I. The relationship between the clearance of the past and salvation:
   A. Clearance of the past not being a requirement for salvation.
   B. Clearance of the past being an issue of the enjoyment of salvation.
   C. Clearance of the past being needed for a better Christian life.

II. The basis of the clearance of the past.

III. Examples of the clearance of the past:
   A. Abandoning idols.
   B. Destroying the demonic and dirty things.
   C. Restoring what we owe.
   D. Ending the old way of living.

IV. The extent of the clearance of the past.

TEXT

After a person is saved, his old way of living and his old conduct of the past should come to an end. Before he received salvation, he was a sinner living in sin. He was also a man of the old creation, behaving in the way of the old creation. But now, having been saved, he has become a man of the new creation with the life of the new creation; as such he should have a new beginning, a new start, and live a new life spontaneously. Therefore, his former living and conduct should be ended.

In the Old Testament, when the children of Israel were saved by their keeping of the Passover, they immediately left Egypt, forsaking all Egyptian ways of living and fully ending, concluding, all the Egyptian things. From that day, the life they lived was new, the way on which they walked was new, and all the things they did were new. The things of the past and the living of the former days were completely ended. This is a distinct type of the clearance of the past.

Although the Bible contains no plain teaching concerning the clearance of the past, it does include some passages that are pertinent to this matter. According to these passages, we may extract the following four points:

I. THE RELATIONSHIP BETWEEN THE CLEARANCE OF THE PAST AND SALVATION

A. Clearance of the Past Not Being a Requirement for Salvation

The clearance of the past is not a requirement for salvation. This is because God's salvation is complete. No matter how grievous or deep our sins might be, they are all under the precious blood. There is no need for us to do or add anything, such as clearing the past, before we can be forgiven by God. God's forgiveness is based upon the precious blood of the Lord Jesus, and it is also the issue of our repentance and faith. It is not necessary to add our good works and virtues or our zeal and love. Therefore, the clearance of the past is not a requirement for salvation.

B. Clearance of the Past
Being an Issue of the Enjoyment of Salvation

Once a person receives the Lord Jesus as his Savior and thus obtains God's salvation, the power of this salvation causes him to clear away and end his former life. This is plainly illustrated in Zaccheus' action as recorded in Luke 19. At the moment God's salvation came to Zaccheus, it caused him to deal with his material possessions and to clear away his past sinful life. In like manner, because of our enjoyment of God's salvation, God's life in us causes us to have a change in our mood, taste, and feeling toward the world. Even our taste toward daily necessities, such as eating and clothing, is changed. Therefore, we spontaneously put an end to our old way of living, that is, we clear away the things in our living which have evolved from the past to the present, no longer allowing them to persist or continue. Such a clearance is an issue of our enjoyment of salvation.

C. Clearance of the Past
Being Needed for a Better Christian Life

Once a person is saved, if he desires to have a good testimony for the Lord and to go on with the Lord in a pure way, he should completely clear away the things of his past. Suppose a casino operator is saved. Of course, his past sin of operating the casino has been forgiven by God. Moreover, the many dark and evil things he did in the casino have also been forgiven. However, if he desires to be a good Christian from now on and to follow and go on with the Lord, he has no choice but to close the casino. If he does not close it down, though we may not deny that he is saved, we may say that he has no way to live as a Christian. If he desires to have a good Christian life, he must close the casino. This is the clearance of the past.

If after he is saved an operator of a casino or a night club does not close down his business, how can he lead people to the Lord or witness for the Lord? Even if he tries to witness for the Lord, it will be difficult for anyone to believe. If after we are saved we desire to walk on the Lord's way and to witness for the Lord, we need to clear away our past life and the former things. We should regard this matter as highly important. This is not a legal requirement, and there is no fixed rule or regulation as to how we should make the clearance. Nevertheless, there is a principle here: if we, the saved ones, desire to have a better Christian life, to walk properly on the way of the Lord, and to witness for the Lord, our past life must be brought to an end.

II. THE BASIS OF THE CLEARANCE OF THE PAST

The clearance of the past is not according to the demand of outward regulations but according to the moving of the Spirit within. The Bible does not have any plain teaching telling us that we should clear the past, nor does it give us any regulation suggesting to us how we should make such a clearance. Since we are saved, however, we have the Spirit in us. If anyone would let the Spirit move and work in him and would not care for his position, reputation, and profit, the Spirit will lead him to make the clearance with all its dealings by the power of life within, that he may be a new man, living a new life and walking on the new way. Furthermore, this clearance is not a regulation in the church. The church has no such regulation or requirement. However, the life we have obtained is holy, and the Spirit in us is moving and working. Hence, the Spirit will definitely require us, by the holy life within us, to remove all demonic and dirty things and to cut off the old way of living. Our responsibility is to follow the leading of the Spirit and to allow Him to move freely.

III. EXAMPLES OF THE CLEARANCE OF THE PAST

Although the Bible has no clear teaching concerning the clearance of the past, the New Testament contains distinct examples showing us that after a man is saved, the Spirit begins to move and work in him, causing him to clear the past and to deal with the improper things of the past.

A. Abandoning Idols

One example of the clearance of the past is seen in the case of the Thessalonians. In 1 Thessalonians 1:9 Paul said that, after they had believed in the Lord, the Thessalonians turned away from idols. Today, especially in places like China and Japan, most of the unbelieving families have idols or things pertaining to idols. After a person is saved, whether he is about to be baptized or has already been baptized, he must clear away from his living the idols and things related to idols. He may not force himself to do other things, but regarding the matter of clearing away the idols, it is all right for a person to force himself a little. If he finds it difficult to do the clearing, he may find some brothers to pray with him in order to increase his strength and boldness and thereby to help him with the clearing. However, he must do the clearing himself, and do it thoroughly, the more thoroughly the better.

Among the Chinese, there are things related to the reading of facial features, fortune-telling, horoscopes, and divination. Since these things involve idols, they should be terminated. It is improper for a believer who has been baptized to have idols or other superstitious things remaining in his home. We must abandon all things that are related to idols. The more severely we forsake them, and the more thoroughly we clean them out, the better.

Not only should we discard the idols that are obvious, but we should reject even the idols that are not obvious. Not only should we throw out other images, but we should give up even portraits or statues of Jesus. All the so-called paintings of Jesus today are false. The Bible says that, when He was on earth, the Lord Jesus had no form nor comeliness (Isa. 53:2). However, the images of Jesus most commonly seen today look very beautiful. These are artists' false portrayals of Jesus. Not only Catholics but even many Protestants have this kind of picture in their homes. Furthermore, many books in Christianity contain such pictures. These pictures represent human superstitions, and in the eyes of God they are blasphemous; hence, they should be disposed of.

We should discard any image of Jesus, not merely because it is false. Even if it were to bear the original semblance of Jesus, it still should be rejected. We should use our spirit to worship the Lord, who is Spirit (John 4:24); we should not use our physical body to worship a visible image. The Catholic church teaches that man should worship a visible image with his physical body in order to help him to worship the invisible God with his inner spirit. This is a heretical teaching which mixes leaven into the fine flour (Matt. 13:33). We should not follow such a teaching. We should worship the Lord in spirit and not have any outward images.

B. Destroying the Demonic and Dirty Things

A second example of the clearance of the past is seen in the case of the Ephesians. Acts 19:19 tells us that the Ephesian believers who practiced magic brought their books together and burned them. This is the basis for our practice of burning for the destruction of the demonic and dirty things, the improper things. Examples of these things are the candlesticks and censers used in idol worship, ornaments and clothing with the image of the dragon, sacred writings of heathen religions, books and charms pertaining to divination, and tablets related to ancestral worship. Other examples are gambling instruments, utensils for alcoholic drinking, pipes for smoking, obscene books, and pornographic pictures. All these things are demonic and filthy. We all must follow the leading of the Holy Spirit to remove all such things from our lives and our homes.

Unbecoming clothing also is in this category of demonic and dirty things. Perhaps some items of clothing are too short; in this case they should be lengthened. Other items may have a peculiar appearance; these items should be altered to appear normal. Still others may be demonic and defiled by sin; such items should be burned. No one can decide the extent of our dealing with these things, but the Spirit will guide us inwardly.

In brief, anything related to idols and any demonic and filthy thing, however valuable it may be, should be burned. The biblical principle is that such things should be burned with fire. The Bible records, in particular, that the price of the items which were burned by the Ephesians was fifty thousand pieces of silver. This is to show us that, when they destroyed the demonic and unclean things, the early believers burned a number of valuable things. Therefore, when we destroy the demonic and dirty things, we should not count the cost or the loss.

C. Restoring What We Owe

A third example of the clearance of the past is seen in the case of Zaccheus, in his restoring of what he owed others. As soon as he was saved, Zaccheus said to the Lord that if he had taken anything from anyone by false accusations, he would restore four times as much (Luke 19:8). To restore four times as much is neither a law nor a principle, but an issue of the dynamic salvation of the Lord, the moving of the Holy Spirit, and the inner urging of the conscience. This sets a good example, disclosing to us the way to deal with material indebtedness.

After we are saved, it is not necessary to dig up our past life to see whom we owe and to repay them. But if the Holy Spirit in us makes us conscious of the fact that we owe others in material things, then we should follow His leading to properly restore them.

As to the way of making restitution, there are a number of practical points that need consideration. First, perhaps at the present time you are financially unable to repay your debts. If you feel that the Holy Spirit is requiring you to deal with the matter immediately, though you cannot make the full restitution, you should still do your best to restore what you owe and confess your sin to the one whom you owe. This is the first point for consideration.

Second, when you restore what you owe, sometimes you should make it known to the party whom you have wronged, but at other times you should exercise wisdom and not let him know. If your making the matter known to him will not benefit everyone involved, then you may restore what you owe in secret. For example, suppose you have stolen something, and the victim knows that it is you who did the stealing. If this is the case, then you must let him know that you are restoring what you stole from him. On the other hand, suppose he is not aware of your wrongdoing, and suppose that by informing him about it you may cause further complication and involve other parties, so that you may create more problems and wrong more people. Under this circumstance, you should simply pay him back in secret so that the victim will not suffer any material loss and at the same time others will not be implicated.

Third, if the person you have wronged is no longer alive, in principle you should reimburse his nearest relative, such as his wife or children. In other words, you should reimburse his legal heirs. If no one can be found to receive the reimbursement, in principle it is best to give the money to the poor.

Fourth, how much should the compensation be? Should it be the amount owed, twice the amount, or several times the amount? Perhaps your feeling is not clear. In such a case, the best thing for you to do is to fellowship with the older ones in the church. In general, try to take the middle course. Avoid underdoing, not doing enough, so that your conscience is still condemned. Also avoid overdoing, doing in excess, so that your conscience is overburdened. There are no fixed regulations on such matters. We must try to do the most suitable thing by carefully weighing the situation and following the leading of the Holy Spirit.

In brief, the restoration of material things should be done with much discretion because it often involves others. Sometimes it may involve the government, at other times it may involve private individuals, and at still other times it may involve the relationship between husband and wife in a family. Therefore, when we carry out such dealings, we should not merely care for the peace of our conscience and our guiltlessness before the Lord and disregard the safety of others. We must avoid putting others in a difficult situation through our dealings. Therefore, we need to exercise wisdom to carry out the dealings properly, so that those whom we have wronged will receive compensation while other parties will not be damaged. We should keep in mind that the underlying principle in restoring what we owe is that the Lord may be glorified and that others may be profited together with us. We must handle the matter of making restitution according to this principle so that no damage will be done to anyone.

D. Ending the Old Way of Living

After we are saved, we should conclude our old way of living. Although we cannot find a definite example in the Bible concerning this point, we can see a hint of it from the revelation of the entire New Testament. That is, after we are saved, God's desire is that we bring before Him every person, thing, and affair in our living and see if we still can be related to them as we were in the former days.

If we are willing to go before the Lord in this way, we will see that after we are saved through regeneration, we not only should abandon the idols, destroy the demonic and dirty things, and restore what we owe, but we also should conclude entirely our old way of living and have a new beginning. Since regeneration causes a new life to be imparted into us, spontaneously it also ushers us into a new living. The old way of living is terminated with the old life, and the new way of living is germinated with the new life. This does not mean that we cease to be husbands, parents, or students; rather, it means that we can no longer be husbands, parents, or students as we were in the past. Neither does it mean that from now on our homes should be devoid of decoration; rather, it means that the decorating should be different from before. Concerning these things, our inward taste, our mood, and our feeling have changed. This means that our old life with our old way of living has been ended.

Such an ending does not require us to dig up the past. It is not a matter of asking ourselves about our wrongdoings in the past; it is a matter of asking ourselves whether we, as children of God, should be the same as before. Some people are saved strongly, and they immediately end their old way of living. Their worldly ambition and interest are changed. Their evaluation and concept of persons, things, and affairs also are changed. Even the purpose of their human life is different from before. Thus, they can rid themselves of all entanglements and remove all the weights that they may press forward on the way of the Lord. This is not a teaching but the work of the Holy Spirit. It is altogether a matter of the new man with a new living, having everything of the past living ended. This is the clearance of the past.

We must bring these four categories of things—things related to idols, demonic and dirty things, things we owe others, and the entire old way of living—before God in order that they may be properly ended. Anyone who does not allow the Spirit to do a proper work in him in these matters cannot go on with the Lord in a proper way. Although dealings with these matters are not based on teaching, law, or regulation, they will surely issue forth if a person lives in the spirit and is worked on by the Spirit.

IV. THE EXTENT OF THE CLEARANCE OF THE PAST

The extent of clearance of the past is the "life and peace" spoken of in Romans 8:6. We have seen that the basis of the ending of the past is the moving of the Spirit, which is the feeling given to us through the inner anointing of the Holy Spirit. If we walk according to the Spirit, the result will surely be life and peace (Rom. 8:5-6). Thus life and peace are the degree to which we are required to clear the past. If we follow the demand of our inner sense to restore what we owe, to confess our sins, to eliminate improper, demonic, and dirty things, and to end our old way of living, we will have the sense that we are strengthened, enlightened, satisfied, and enlivened; we will also have the sense of peace, security, and God's full presence. If we have made a clearance of the things of the past and we still sense the lack of fullness and manifestation of life and peace, we may be sure that we have not followed the Spirit to the uttermost; we have not sufficiently satisfied the demand of the inner feeling. We must look to the Lord for the supply of grace that we may clear up things more thoroughly, until we are full of life and peace.

The sense of life and peace within is not sufficient, of course, to prove that all our past that needs to be cleared up has already been dealt with. It only indicates that we have attended to everything according to the demand of our inner feeling. It is possible that later, when the life within has grown and our consciousness has increased, we will sense that there is more that needs to be put to an end. At this time we must again follow the leading of this feeling and deal with these matters until we again sense life and peace. After several thorough clearances and dealings, we will have cleared away to a much greater extent those things, deeds, relations, and concepts of the past which are not pleasing to the Lord. We can then follow the Lord and go on without hindrance.

SUMMARY

The clearance of the past after we are saved refers to the ending of our former living and past conduct. This is not a requirement for salvation, but an issue of the enjoyment of salvation. It is needed in order that we may have a better Christian life, bear a good testimony for the Lord, and follow the Lord in our going on with Him. The practice of the clearance of the past is not according to the demand of outward regulations, but according to the moving of the Spirit within. If we would let the Spirit work in us, He will lead us to make the clearance and carry out the dealings by the power of life within. Although the Bible has no clear teaching concerning the clearance of the past, the New Testament contains some distinct examples: 1) abandoning idols and things pertaining to idols; 2) destroying the demonic, dirty, and improper things; 3) restoring what we owe; and 4) ending the old way of living. These will certainly issue forth if we live in the spirit and are worked on by the Spirit. The extent of clearance of the past is life and peace. We must thoroughly make such a clearance and carry out such dealings until we are inwardly filled with life and peace.

QUESTIONS

1. State briefly the relationship between the clearance of the past and salvation.

2. State briefly the basis of the clearance of the past.

3. Review briefly the biblical examples of the clearance of the past.

4. Explain briefly the extent of the clearance of the past.